"Once you start reading Philip Greene's new book, be warned: You're going to want to drop everything and jet off to Paris to drink classic cocktails and chase the ghosts of Hemingway and Fitzgerald."

—Noah Rothbaum, author of *The Art of American Whiskey* and editor of *The Daily Beast*'s "Half Full" food and drink section

"A unique, informative and entertaining perspective of Paris during the Roaring Twenties, a city literally brimming over with creativity. You've done it again Philip, I think I'll have another!"

—Christopher Struble, president of the Michigan Hemingway Society

"If there ever was a time and place I'd travel back to in a heartbeat it would be Paris in the early 1900s. The romance, the banter, the comradery, the fun—and, of course, the drinks. Philip Greene brings it all to life in this book, so now I can read and I can dream, and I can almost touch that absinthe spoon of years gone by. The past lies in this book. And what a glorious past it is."

—Gary "Gaz" Regan, author of *The Joy of Mixology*

"Paris in the 1920s has always held a fascination for cocktail drinkers and for lovers of great literature. Fortunately, Philip Greene is both. He mixes a wonderful tale, using cocktails as a prism to view this golden moment in place and time. You'll be transported to a table with Hemingway, Fitzgerald, and Stein, with a glass in hand, in a lovely story that will stay with you wherever you go."

—Jacob Briars, global advocacy director for Bacardi

"Just as fans of Philip Greene were recovering from overindulging in *To Have and Have Another*, his great guide for Hemingway cocktail connoisseurs, comes another round guaranteed to topple us off the wagon as we tipple through it. From absinthe to the Whiskey Sour, Greene's chapters offer an intoxicating mix of history, anecdotes, and recipes. This book is a must-have for Lost Generation fans, allowing us to taste-test our way through the literature and lifestyle of an era and a place that always leaves us thirsting for more."

—KIRK CURNUTT, PHD, AUTHOR OF *A READER'S GUIDE TO HEMINGWAY'S TO HAVE AND HAVE NOT* AND VICE PRESIDENT OF THE F. SCOTT FITZGERALD SOCIETY

"Philip Greene has a successful family life, professional life, and a well-documented passion: the life and favorite drinks of Ernest Hemingway. From that base, Philip has expanded his scope to include the other famous, and often infamous, denizens of 1920s Paris. Hemingway and his coterie embraced that continuous *fil conducteur*, that of drinking, the places to go, the people to meet, and what to drink in their presence. More than anyone, Philip is familiar with all these facets, many of which shined in Paris."

—COLIN PETER FIELD, HEAD BARTENDER AT THE BAR HEMINGWAY, PARIS RITZ AND AUTHOR OF *THE COCKTAILS OF THE PARIS RITZ*

"This book has been a real time capsule for me, giving a lot of context from the period, including the great opportunities to (re)discover some cocktails, bars, and Parisian streets."

—FERNANDO CASTELLON, DRINK HISTORIAN

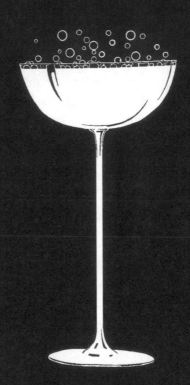

A DRINKABLE FEAST

A Cocktail Companion

to 1920s Paris

PHILIP GREENE

A TarcherPerigee Book

tarcherperigee

AN IMPRINT OF PENGUIN RANDOM HOUSE LLC
375 Hudson Street
New York, New York 10014

Most TarcherPerigee books are available at special quantity discounts for bulk
purchase for sales promotions, premiums, fund-raising, and educational needs.
Special books or book excerpts also can be created to fit specific needs. For details,
write: SpecialMarkets@penguinrandomhouse.com.

LIBRARY OF CONGRESS CATALOGING-IN-PUBLICATION DATA
Names: Greene, Philip, 1961–author.
Title: A drinkable feast : a cocktail companion to 1920s Paris / Philip Greene.
Description: New York, New York : TarcherPerigee Book, [2018] | Includes
bibliographical references and index. |
Identifiers: LCCN 2018018496 (print) | LCCN 2018018990 (ebook) |
ISBN 9780525504849 | ISBN 9780143133018 (alk. paper)
Subjects: LCSH: Cocktails. | LCGFT: Cookbooks.
Classification: LCC TX951 (ebook) | LCC TX951 .G782 2018 (print) |
DDC 641.87/4—dc23
LC record available at https://lccn.loc.gov/2018018496
p.   cm.

Printed in the United States of America

3rd Printing

Book design by Sabrina Bowers

TO HANNAH,
MADELEINE, AND OLIVIA

CONTENTS

FOREWORD

WITH *A DRINKABLE FEAST: A COCKTAIL COMPANION to 1920s Paris*, Phil Greene has written a memorable book for those of us who love to drink, love Paris, and who at some point have ever wondered what it would have been like to live in a city with artists such as Pablo Picasso, F. Scott Fitzgerald, Gertrude Stein, Joan Miró, James Joyce, Josephine Baker, Man Ray, Ezra Pound, and Ernest Hemingway, to name but a few. Phil's answer is that either as a tourist or as a young writer fleeing Prohibition-era America, in Paris you would have been drinking—and drinking a lot. Alcohol and, in particular, the cocktails served in the American bars that were showing up all over Paris during the 1920s, were the spark that fired the creative juices of the Lost Generation. It was their social drug of choice, and in this book Phil uses more than fifty cocktail recipes, including everything from Absinthe to the Buñueloni to Grog Americain (a favorite of my grandfather) and the Monkey Gland (a drink that claimed to have restorative, Viagra-like properties), to give us his *fresco* of this remarkable period.

Two of the principal reasons for the enormous influx of Americans to *La Ville Lumière* during the twenties were the Volstead Act and the fantastic exchange rate for anyone coming to France with US dollars. The Volstead Act, aka Prohibition, became the law of the land in America on January 17, 1920, meaning that if you wanted to drink you either had to find a speakeasy or quit the United States. For those who opted for the latter, the relative strength of the dollar throughout that decade made living the life of a poor, struggling artist in Paris neither poor nor all that difficult (my grandfather Ernest included). In his memoir, *A Moveable Feast*, Hemingway wrote nostalgically about "how Paris was in the early days when we were very poor and very happy," but Ernest certainly wasn't starving. Phil points out that while a bottle of imported whiskey was certainly prohibitive for the average working-class Frenchman, it was relatively cheap for an American armed with dollars. Indeed, my grandfather and his wife Hadley lived quite well on her modest trust fund and the small amount of money that he earned as a journalist for the *Toronto Star*.

Paris was not just inexpensive, it was also a city of freedom. In this case, freedom included the ability to drink where you wanted without being hassled by the police. But also in the case of black Americans, it meant the freedom of being treated as equals. Phil highlights the fact that it was quite normal to see interracial couples in Paris and that some of the best jazz bands of the era were found in the bars of Montparnasse, because that was where they were given the respect they merited as artists and where they were treated as normal human beings no different from anyone else.

Women, too, found it a very congenial place to be. In Paris, women were not just the wives of important men but artists, entertainers, and writers in their own right who had a tremendous impact on the culture of the twentieth century. For example, where would James Joyce be today without Sylvia Beach, the owner of the legendary bookstore Shakespeare and Company and the publisher of Joyce's magnum opus, *Ulysses*? Or, for that matter, what of the many painters—Pablo Picasso in particular—who benefitted from the financial patronage of Gertrude Stein? Of course, everyone knows that Stein, along with Ezra Pound, was one of the early mentors of my grandfather. Yet, I am not at all sure that Ernest Hemingway's many admirers realize how much he took from this woman. Many years ago, I remember hearing that Ernest would show her his short stories and that she would look at them and tell him what was good and what wasn't, and then he would go back to the little apartment, where he wrote, and work on them until they met with her approval. Later on, when I was working on my memoir, *Strange Tribe*, I read that it was Gertrude Stein who first suggested that Ernest travel to Pamplona during the

Fiesta to see the running of the bulls and the *corrida* because she knew that as an artist it was something that he had to understand and experience. Still, it wasn't until I had finished my memoir that I realized the depth of his debt to her as a writer. One day, a friend of mine was reading a book and she said, "John, listen to this and tell me who you think it is." So I listened to her read a paragraph that seemed vaguely familiar, and when she finished I told her, "Obvious. It's Ernest." No, she told me, it was Gertrude Stein's and she had written it in 1901, when my grandfather was two years old. I was stunned by the similarity in styles. Indeed, throughout my reading of Phil's book I was constantly reminded with his references to Stein, Ezra Pound, Fitzgerald, and the many others who influenced his writing that without Paris, there never would have been an Ernest Hemingway— at least not the one that we all know today.

Now that I think about it, perhaps Phil has done us all a great favor in writing *A Drinkable Feast*, though I doubt he is aware of it. His passion for Paris in the twenties recalls not only the cocktails of that time and the people who made and drank them, but also everything about that era that was crazy and wonderful, over the top and sublime all at once. In short, he captures the vitality, beauty, and creative effervescence of Paris perfectly.

You could almost say that Phil has written a subversive book and not just a cocktail companion. Why? Because by shining a spotlight on the Paris of the 1920s and the expats and Frenchmen who created this monument to freedom, excess, and the art of drinking well, he inevitably forces us to make comparisons with the present and the culture that we have today. Perhaps not everyone will read the book the way that I am reading it, but I do know from the twenty years I spent in Milan as a young man how gradual and hard to perceive this change in perspective can be. You start out thinking like an American, and then before you know it you're something else, neither American nor Italian. You've become an expat, and that is the first step toward a different point of view and a new kind of freedom.

Of course, if you want you can always skip the vignettes and histories regarding the cocktails and the artists and head straight for the drinks. The recipes are all there, but something tells me that many of you will be subtly seduced by *A Drinkable Feast*, and that under the influence of a Dôme Cocktail, a Bronx, or a Jimmie Special, you will hear the siren call of the surrealists and the Lost Generation and never look back.

JOHN HEMINGWAY
Montreal, 2018

INTRODUCTION

"**P**ARIS WAS WHERE THE TWENTIETH CENTURY WAS." SO
said Gertrude Stein of the City of Light in the 1920s. It was a
mecca for a wide range of artists, writers, composers and musicians,
poets, dancers and choreographers, architects, fashion designers,
and, lastly, hangers-on, poseurs, and the inevitable tourists. All of
them added flavor, style, innovation, and nuance to the international
cocktail that was Paris.

They came to Paris for a variety of reasons, and each new arrival
contributed to a snowball effect that attracted more to follow. The list of
those living in or visiting Paris reads like a cultural who's who, includ-
ing: Ernest Hemingway, F. Scott and Zelda Fitzgerald, James Joyce,
John Dos Passos, E. E. Cummings, George Orwell, Ezra Pound, Man
Ray, Josephine Baker, Sara and Gerald Murphy, Robert McAlmon,
Django Reinhardt, Djuna Barnes, William Faulkner, Cole Porter, Harry
and Caresse Crosby, William Carlos Williams, Waldo Peirce, Langston
Hughes, James Thurber, William Shirer, Salvador Dalí, Coco Chanel,
Pablo Picasso, Sylvia Beach, Gertrude Stein, Jean Cocteau, Dorothy
Parker, Edna St. Vincent Millay, George Gershwin, Edmund Wilson,
T. S. Eliot, Robert Benchley, and many others. They came to Paris,
yearning to be free and to create. These included the surrealists, the
modernists, the members of the Lost Generation. They found suste-
nance and inspiration in the city's cafés, bars, restaurants, cabarets, art
galleries, and gardens, from Montmartre to Montparnasse, and along
the Champs-Élysées and boulevard Saint-Germain.

I'm probably no different from any other English major (ahem,
English *minor*) who was introduced to the Lost Generation and captivated by the magic of the era. In these pages, I hope to share some

of the reasons why I, and so many others, find this era so utterly compelling.

I'm further hopeful of shedding new light on the epoch by viewing it through a different lens: the stories of the cocktails, cafés, and cabarets of Paris in the 1920s. What were the favorite drinks of these brightest lights in the City of Light? What were the popular watering holes? What stories can be told of these legendary days and endless nights, what the French labeled *les années folles*, "the crazy years," and what F. Scott Fitzgerald termed "the greatest, gaudiest spree in history"?

In his memoir, *A Moveable Feast*, you'll find Hemingway's oft-quoted comment: "If you are lucky enough to have lived in Paris as a young man, then wherever you go for the rest of your life, it stays with you, for Paris is a moveable feast." Perhaps this book might aid in your enjoyment of Paris, evoking that golden era, even if you've never been.

As an aside, please understand that within the four corners of a cocktail book there are things I am going to miss, and things I don't delve into. Don't be disappointed if I don't explain the differences between Dadaism and surrealism. That said, the fear of missing anyone or anything from that era kept me up many nights. Oh no, did I mention André Breton or Sacco and Vanzetti? There, I just did.

In the pages to follow, I'll share with you some of the more popular and interesting drinks of the day, and some notable tales that go with them. And you'll learn how to make these drinks at home. After all, as a Hemingway character put it, "That's all we do, isn't it—look at things and try new drinks?"

Why Paris?

You've heard me say it, and you likely heard your English professor say it: Paris was the cultural epicenter of the Western world in the 1920s. But why? Because so many notable people were there. That sounds flippant but it's true, and if we examine the types of people who came to Paris, we can get a better sense as to their motivations. We can also learn a great deal about why they left home, particularly "expat" Americans, and especially those who came of age during World War I, the so-called Lost Generation.

This term was said to have been coined by Gertrude Stein, circa 1923. She'd witnessed an exasperated garage owner berating his young mechanic. He considered the mechanic's entire age group as a *"génération perdue,"* a lost generation. Recounting it to Hemingway, Stein agreed, saying, "That's what you all are. All of you young people who served in the war. You are a lost generation. . . . You have no respect for anything. You drink yourselves to death." Hemingway quoted her in the prologue to his 1926 novel, *The Sun Also Rises*; the label stuck, and it came to be applied to all those who'd been scarred and disillusioned by World War I.

Of these so-called lost youths who migrated to Paris were those from the literary world—the poets, writers, and publishers. Poet Archibald MacLeish called the era the "greatest period of literary and artistic innovation since the Renaissance." Hemingway called Paris "the town best organized for a writer to write in that there is." It was the era of independent publishing houses and "little magazines": Bill Bird's Three Mountains Press; Robert McAlmon's Contact Editions; Margaret Anderson and Eugene Jolas's *Transition*; Jane Heap and Ezra Pound's *The Little Review* (though published in New York City); Ethel Moorhead, E. W. Titus; and Ernest Walsh's *This Quarter*; Ford Madox Ford's *The Transatlantic Review*; Florence Gilliam and Arthur Moss's *Gargoyle*. All were dedicated to publishing new and creative works, and all attracted rich talent to Paris. There were also three American newspapers in Paris: the *Paris Herald Tribune* (*New York Herald Tribune*), the *Paris Times*, and the *Paris Tribune* (*Chicago Tribune*).

Many expat Americans were repulsed not only by the carnage of war but also by what they saw taking place in America, notably Prohibition. "Many returning soldiers found American life empty of meaning and looked back at Europe with longing. Harry Crosby, who had served as an ambulance driver in the thick of battle, found postwar America bleak and depressing."

Poet Ezra Pound left the States because he'd grown disgusted with the "enfeebled or adolescent Amurkn mind." Others sensed a

*Four of the titans of the Paris literary and publishing world: Ezra
Pound, John Quinn, Ford Madox Ford, and James Joyce.*
PHOTOGRAPH COURTESY OF THE POETRY COLLECTION OF THE
UNIVERSITY LIBRARIES, UNIVERSITY AT BUFFALO, THE STATE
UNIVERSITY OF NEW YORK.

pronounced "strain of Puritanism." Writer Malcolm Cowley eloquently described it as "the idea of salvation by exile. 'They do things
better in Europe: let's go there.'"

Henry Miller would write, "I love it here, I want to stay forever. . . .
I will write here, I will live and write alone. And each day I want to see
a little more of Paris, study it, learn it as I would a book. . . . The
streets sing, the stones talk. The houses drip history, glory, romance."
William Faulkner observed, "Paris for us young fry was good as the
sun on your back, an eager look at things you maybe felt had mean-
ings you didn't get from the folks back at the store." Canadian writer
Morley Callaghan agreed: "Looking back on it, what American writer
of the 20s or 30s, or the 50s, from Gertrude Stein to Faulkner to
Henry Miller or Tennessee Williams didn't feel compelled to drop
into the great style center to look around?"

Perhaps Gertrude Stein said it best: "It was not so much what

France gave you, it was what she did not take away ... So," she continued, "Paris was the place that suited those of us that were to create the twentieth century art and literature, naturally enough."

Stein was a shining example of another category of expat: the empowered women. In addition to writing, they would establish artistic and literary salons, as Stein and Natalie Barney did. These salons hosted the brightest lights of the literary and artistic world. Further, Stein, her brother Leo, and her companion Alice B. Toklas became renowned collectors of art. Their salon at 27 rue de Fleurus was adorned with works of Pablo Picasso, Paul Cézanne, Paul Gauguin, Pierre-Auguste Renoir, Henri de Toulouse-Lautrec, and many others. At Barney's salon, the "Temple of Friendship," at 20 rue Jacob, "always, champagne and cocktails flowed generously."

Barney was one of many women who felt freer in Paris with respect to lifestyle, "and if she had explained, she might have agreed with Willa Cather: 'the United States has gotten ahead wonderfully, but somehow ahead on the wrong road.'"

Women also played an important role in publishing. In addition to Anderson, Heap, and Moorhead, Sylvia Beach and her companion Adrienne Monnier were both significant stewards of Paris's literary community. With complementary bookstores on rue de l'Odéon, Beach's Shakespeare and Company (English-language offerings) and Monnier's La Maison des Amis des Livres (French) not only sold and loaned books but also published them. Beach courageously funded and printed Joyce's controversial *Ulysses* in 1922, and Monnier was the first to translate Hemingway into French in 1926, as well as works of Walt Whitman, William Carlos Williams, Robert McAlmon, E. E. Cummings, and others. Women were also prominent patrons of the arts, notably Peggy Guggenheim and Nancy Cunard.

Women in Paris could, for the most part, drink side by side with men. As noted by Paul Cohen-Portheim, "The London bar is intended exclusively for the male sex; whereas this only applies to one among the more important ones in Paris, namely the Ritz Bar, which is an Anglo-American reserve. In all the others—whether it be

Fouquet's, the Sélect on the Champs-Élysées in the west, the Scribe, the Bar de Paris, the Crillon, the New York, the Bodega or the Adega in the center; the Coupole, the Sélect or the Dôme in Montparnasse— both sexes are equally at home."

Henry Miller would remark upon the sense of equality and non-conformity across the board. "Here is the greatest congregation of bizarre types. People do dress as they please, wear beards if they like, and shave if they choose. You don't feel the lifeless pressure of dull regimentation as in N.Y. and London."

African Americans also flocked to Paris, largely around Montmartre's jazz and nightclub scene. Many had served in a US Army band and came to discover that, in France, which had abolished slavery long before the United States, "blacks were treated as well as whites." While most were entertainers, notably Ada "Bricktop" Smith, Josephine Baker (called *La Bakair* by the adoring French), Eugene Bullard, Sidney Bechet, Florence Jones, Buddy Gilmore, Elisabeth

Le Fouquet's restaurant, 99 Champs-Élysées. When "able to spend money he didn't have, James Joyce liked to eat here whenever he could—which he did with increasing frequency in the late twenties and thirties." VINTAGE POSTCARD FROM THE AUTHOR'S COLLECTION.

* Arlen J. Hansen, *Expatriate Paris* (New York: Arcade, 1990), 220.

Welch, Dooley Wilson, and too many others to count, poet Langston Hughes lived there in 1926 and worked as a dishwasher at Le Grand Duc. In *Harlem in Montmartre: A Paris Jazz Story Between the Great Wars*, William A. Shack referred to this era as the "Paris Harlem Renaissance." Even the 1927 guidebook *Paris with the Lid Lifted* observed that there was "no color line in Paris."

Author John Baxter noted, "The arrival in Paris of black musicians coincided with an influx of tourists who, particularly after the imposition of Prohibition in 1920, flooded its bars, restaurants, and brothels, demanding cocktails and entertainment. For any club that expected to attract foreign clientele, a *bar Americain* with a black bartender and a jazz band, entirely African-American, were indispensable."

Novelist Sherwood Anderson noted that the United States, despite being a so-called melting pot, had become a land of racial intolerance. Paris was far more cosmopolitan. "One often sees negroes dining in restaurants and walking about in the streets with their white sweethearts. The sight attracts no attention. In an American city it would cause a riot."

In addition to Paris's jazz scene, composer Cole Porter was there, and George Gershwin wrote his classic *An American in Paris* there in 1928, which included actual Parisian taxi horns. Also in Paris were Arthur Rubinstein and Maurice Chevalier, as well as a group of French composers known as Les Six: Darius Milhaud, Georges Auric, Louis Durey, Arthur Honegger, Francis Poulenc, and Germaine Tailleferre, with Jean Cocteau as its informal "spokesman." American composer George Antheil, who lived upstairs of Sylvia Beach's shop, would compose and present his controversial 1924 *Ballet Mécanique* in Paris.

The world of ballet and contemporary dance was also well represented, notably Isadora Duncan, Serge Diaghilev, Igor Stravinsky and the Ballets Russes. Paris also attracted innovative filmmakers, photographers, and other artists of multiple media, such as Berenice Abbott, Man Ray, Luis Buñuel, Jean Cocteau, Fernand Léger, and Mario Nalpas. Of course, you had the artists, Pablo Picasso, Salvador Dalí, Chaïm Soutine, Tsuguharu Foujita, Moïse Kisling, Juan Gris,

Thelma Wood, Joan Miró, Francis Picabia, Constantin Brâncuşi, Amedeo Modigliani, and far, far too many others to list here. Joined by pioneering architects such as Le Corbusier, they were all determined to "make it new."

In addition to the various arts noted above, Paris became a mecca for the cocktail arts. Indeed, the iconic cocktail glassware of René Lalique, including the classic V-shaped glass we now know as the "Martini glass," was displayed at the Exposition Internationale des Arts Décoratifs et Industriels Modernes, held in Paris in 1925.

And, for all the aforementioned reasons, tourists flocked to Paris, many perhaps looking for a good drink. Guidebooks were quick to remind visitors that "Prohibition is three thousand miles away," which meant that "with no violent shock to our principles" one can enjoy "a wee drop of something." But another guide cautioned the tourist, "Don't try to drink Paris dry the first day." That goes for this book, too!

As painter Kees van Dongen would note, the era "should be known as the Cocktail Epoch." Al Laney of the *Paris Herald Tribune* agreed; after all, "society itself as a bright mixture in which were blended people of all tastes and classes. By all means, 'l'Epoque du Coqutèle'" would be the appropriate name for the age.

For a full list of sources used in this book, please visit ADrinkable Feast.com.

THE
DRINKS

OF COURSE, THERE WERE MANY MORE DRINKS BEING
served in Paris during the 1920s than you'll find in this
volume, not to mention many other noteworthy people and places of
that time. This book is a distillation of the most popular and interesting drinks, and those that brought with them the best stories and
connections to the notable people and places of the era. Of the many
tales of Paris from this glorious era, here are a few. I hope you enjoy.

ABSINTHE (DRIPPED)

> **1 ounce absinthe**
> **1 cube sugar**
> **3–5 ounces ice water (depending on desired strength)**
>
> ---
>
> This drink requires a slotted absinthe spoon and an iced water dispenser with a drip spout. Place the spoon atop a small glass of absinthe, and a sugar cube atop the spoon. Slowly drip the iced water onto the sugar so that it dissolves into the absinthe.

ABSINTHE IS A HIGH-PROOF, DISTILLED SPIRIT, FLAVORED with a variety of herbs, chiefly wormwood (*Artemisia absinthium*), anise, hyssop, fennel, and coriander. It is said to have been invented in the 1790s by a French physician named Pierre Ordinaire. He lived as a refugee of the French Revolution in the Swiss commune of Couvet. Absinthe was outlawed throughout most of the Western world from approximately 1915 to 2007, mainly due to unfounded claims that its active ingredient, thujone, was hallucinogenic and toxic.

Absinthe was very popular in the late nineteenth century, particularly among poets, writers, artists, and bohemians. Its notable devotees included Paul Verlaine, Arthur Rimbaud, Vincent van Gogh, Alfred de Musset, Henri de Toulouse-Lautrec, Paul Gauguin, O. Henry, Oscar Wilde, and many others. The drink's green hue inspired the name *La Fée Verte*, "the Green Fairy." Paintings by artists such as Édouard Manet and Edgar Degas depicted the green-colored temptress, or its dissipating effects on its consumers.

During absinthe's long ban, the void was filled by a wormwood-free absinthe-substitute, known as anise (*anis* in French).* Further, since absinthe was never outlawed in Spain (it was made in the Catalonian city of Tarragona, for example), it remained available, though scarce—kind of like how Cuban rum or cigars have been in the United States since Castro. So, between pre-ban supplies and Spanish sources, there was absinthe in 1920s Paris.

Ernest Hemingway was an absinthe drinker. As a columnist for the *Toronto Daily Star* (now just the *Toronto Star*), he offered a tongue-in-cheek story in 1922 titled "The Great 'Apéritif' Scandal." It seems a product called Anis Del Oso was discovered to be true absinthe. "It had the familiar licorice taste, . . . turned milky when water was added— and it had the slow, culminating wallop that made the boulevardier want to get up and jump on his new straw hat in ecstasy after the third Delloso [*sic*]." But once the law moved in, its makers were forced to reduce it to a common anise. Hemingway sadly noted, "The boulevardier waits in vain for the feeling that makes him want to shinny rapidly up the side of the Eiffel Tower—for it is not absinthe any more." As an aside, poet T. S. Eliot was also a big fan of Anis Del Oso.

The bars and cafés of Paris took the ban seriously, to an extent. As of 1920, one paper noted, "Not a single bar within four miles of the Opera will risk its license by serving an absinthe frappé or putting an absinthe kick in your martini. But many a friendly barman will tell you where to buy all the absinthe you need to drive you crazy for less than $4 a bottle."

In Hemingway's *For Whom the Bell Tolls*, protagonist Robert Jordan uses absinthe to magically transport him from the horrors of the Spanish Civil War back to Paris:

> One cup of it took the place . . . of all the old evenings in cafés, of all chestnut trees that would be in bloom now in this month, . . . of book

---

* See also Pernod Cocktail (page 152).

Vintage Pernod ad. IMAGE COURTESY OF PERNOD RICARD USA.

shops, of kiosks, and of galleries . . . and of being able to read and relax in the evening; of all the things he had enjoyed and forgotten and that came back to him when he tasted that opaque, bitter, tongue-numbing, brain-warming, stomach-warming, idea-changing liquid alchemy.

You'll also find absinthe in Hemingway's 1926 novel, *The Sun Also Rises*. The characters have traveled from Paris to Pamplona, Spain, to attend the fiesta of San Fermin. Protagonist Jake Barnes and his friend Bill Gorton have gone to the café after the day's bullfight and "watched the beginning of the evening of the last night of the fiesta. The absinthe made everything seem better. I drank it without sugar in the dripping glass, and it was pleasantly bitter."

Hemingway was something of a common denominator with absinthe. Poet and publisher Harry Crosby wrote of a 1927 trip to

Pamplona, where he had "cold beer in tall glasses (later on cold absinthe in tall glasses) and Hemingway . . . drove past in a carriage and shouted at us and Waldo Peirce was with him looking like Walt Whitman and everyone began rushing off for the Bullfight (one last round of absinthe) . . ." Crosby had noted in an earlier diary entry that "Hemingway could drink us under the table."

Fellow writer (and occasional Hemingway drinking buddy) James Joyce included absinthe in his 1922 masterpiece, *Ulysses*. In one scene, his character Leopold Bloom excused the behavior of another: "He doesn't know what he's saying. Taken a little more than is good for him. Absinthe. Greeneyed [*sic*] monster." Another scene recalls "a fellow I knew once in Barcelona, queer fellow, used to call it his postprandial. . . . His breath hangs over our saucestained [*sic*] plates, the green fairy's fang thrusting between his lips."

Poet and occultist Aleister Crowley, whom Hemingway dubbed "The Devil's Disciple" and was commonly known as "The Wickedest Man in the World," was also quite the absinthe drinker. His favorite Paris watering hole was "the upstairs drinking room at a restaurant called Le Chat Blanc on the Rue d'Odessa," where he'd often meet English novelist Somerset Maugham. One evening, being the wicked practical joker that he was, Crowley offered some advice to his poet friend Victor Neuburg on what was safe to drink in Paris: "He had been warned against drinking absinthe and we told him that was quite right, but (we added) many other drinks in Paris are terribly dangerous, especially to a nice young man like you; there is only one really, say, mild, harmless beverage and you can drink as much of that as you like, without running the slightest risk, and what you say when you want it is 'Garcon! Un Pernod!'"

Perhaps poet Hart Crane best summed up not only the sensation of absinthe but of the entire era, describing those heady days as "dinners, soirées, poets, erratic millionaires, painters, translations, lobsters, absinthe, music, promenades, oysters, sherry, aspirin, pictures, Sapphic heiresses, editors, books, sailors. And how!"

☞ **TASTING NOTE:** Absinthe is one of those love-it-or-hate-it drinks. If you are a fan of black licorice, you should enjoy it. You might want to dilute it a bit more at first, to get your taste buds acclimated.

ALASKA COCKTAIL

2 ounces Nicholson Original London dry gin*
1 ounce Yellow Chartreuse

Stir well with ice, then strain into a chilled cocktail glass.

Recipe from ABC of Mixing Cocktails *(1930).*

THIS DRINK WAS FAIRLY POPULAR IN 1920s PARIS, AND the earliest recipe comes from the immortal *Barflies and Cocktails*, written by Harry MacElhone (owner of Harry's New York Bar), illustrated by Wynn Holcomb, and including "slight contributions from Arthur Moss."

Not merely a drink for Harry's expat crowd, the Alaska is also found in the 1929 book *Cocktails de Paris* by Georges Gabriel Thenon (under the nom de plume RIP), as well as in the 1930 classic *The Savoy Cocktail Book* by Harry Craddock. Craddock described the Alaska with typical cheek: "So far as can be ascertained, this delectable potion is NOT the staple diet of the Esquimaux. It was probably first thought of in South Carolina—hence its name."

One particular American who enjoyed the Alaska was the poet and publisher Harry Crosby, the quite wealthy nephew of billionaire J. P. Morgan Jr. He worked at the family-owned bank, Morgan, Harjes & Co. That is, until New Year's Eve 1923, when he quit the banking biz to pursue the arts, not to mention a rather decadent lifestyle. Harry

---

* This brand, mentioned by name in the recipe, has only recently been revived.

and his wife, Caresse, founded Black Sun Press, which produced high-quality works from notable authors, including Ernest Hemingway, D. H. Lawrence, James Joyce, Archibald MacLeish, Kay Boyle, Ezra Pound, and others. The couple entertained lavishly, often in bed and/or in their spacious bathtub, with endless cocktails, Champagne, and caviar. They were particularly obsessed with horse racing and owned a not-too-successful horse named Gin-Cocktail. They also staged drunken polo matches (on donkeys, not horses). Hemingway observed that "Harry has a wonderful gift of carelessness, he can just spill the stuff out," referring to his poetry, I presume.

In September 1929, it seems Harry had bet heavily on the St Leger Stakes, one of Britain's oldest horse races. He'd put his money on a

Harry and Caresse Crosby, on their wedding day, September 9, 1922. PHOTOGRAPH COURTESY OF THE SPECIAL COLLECTIONS RESEARCH CENTER, MORRIS LIBRARY, SOUTHERN ILLINOIS UNIVERSITY.

horse named Hotweed. The odds were 6–1, and if Hotweed won, "all the wasted months of gambling will be refunded in a day." His journal read: "All morning getting more and more nervous about Hotweed is he going to win is he going to win . . ." Anxiously, Harry took "three spoonfuls from the bottle marked Passifloreine [*sic*]." It seemed to calm him, but when friends arrived for lunch, "we all drank Alaska cocktails 2/3 gin and 1/3 yellow chartreuse I began to feel stimulated and excited again." Unfortunately, his elation would not last; Hotweed ran a bad race, and Harry lost one hundred pounds, bringing his total for that year to about $2,500 lost after converting to dollars.

In case you're wondering, passiflorine is an herbal medicine, commonly used in the 1920s for nerves. While reading this passage, I can't help but be reminded of the comment of T. S. Eliot: when asked what gave him his inspiration to write such vivid poetry, he replied, "Gin and drugs, madam, gin and drugs."

☞ **TASTING NOTE:** The Alaska is a nice variation on the classic Dry Martini, and a good introduction to the herbal liqueur Chartreuse. If you can't find Nicholson Original gin, try any good London dry gin, such as Fords or Citadelle. Oddly enough, this exact same drink is called the Webster F. Street Lay-Away Plan in John Steinbeck's 1954 novel, *Sweet Thursday.*

AMERICANO

1 ounce Campari
1 ounce sweet vermouth
1 ounce seltzer water
Orange or lemon, for garnish

Add all ingredients to a wineglass or a rocks glass filled with ice, stir. Garnish with the peel of an orange or lemon, or with a slice of orange.

Recipe from 900 Recettes de Cocktails et Boissons Americaines *(1927).*

WHILE TYPICALLY THOUGHT OF AS AN ITALIAN DRINK, the Americano was popular in 1920s Paris. Along with this recipe, you'll find it in Frank Meier's *The Artistry of Mixing Drinks*, suggesting that he added it to the Paris Ritz Bar repertoire between 1921 and 1936.

Among the many Americano recipes in 1920s France—an interesting version is in *370 Recettes de Cocktails* by Jean Lupoiu (1928), with equal parts Campari, Aperitivo Rossi, Cinzano sweet vermouth, and seltzer water, and garnished with a lemon peel. It's interesting to see two different apéritif bitters in one drink, and I've tried it with both Campari and Peychaud's Aperitivo, which makes for a nice change.

The drink captures the spirit of the classic Parisian apéritif, in that it contains relatively low-alcohol components and is cut with seltzer water, making it quite suitable for long hours on café terraces. Author Ian Fleming twice had James Bond enjoying the Americano, and

Cover of the 1927 book 900 Recettes de Cocktails et Boissons Americaines. IMAGE COURTESY OF EXPOSITION UNIVERSELLE DES VINS ET SPIRITUEUX.

both times in France.* In fact, as Bond enjoyed one at Fouquet's, on the Champs-Élysées, we learn of Fleming's views on drinking in Paris. He chose the Americano because "one cannot drink seriously in French cafés. . . . No, in cafés you have to drink the least offensive of the musical comedy drinks that go with them, and Bond always had the same thing—an Americano—Bitter Campari, Cinzano, a large slice of lemon peel and soda. For the soda he always specified Perrier, for in his opinion expensive soda water was the cheapest way to improve a poor drink."

---

* In *Casino Royale* and "From a View to a Kill."

I can't help but think that Fleming must have read the 1930 guide-book *How to Wine and Dine in Paris*, which echoed his misgivings:

Ordinarily one in search of a cocktail should take it in an American bar and not order it on a café terrace—even on the terraces of the big boulevard cafés down-town. For the barmen in these bourgeois places are apt to have queer ideas about the way to mix a cocktail.

☞ **TASTING NOTE:** The Americano offers an excellent platform for experimenting with the use of different expressions of vermouth and apéritif bitters, or even a quinquina (such as L.N. Mattei Cap Corse) in place of the vermouth. For example, Suze, Peychaud's Aperitivo, or Cocchi Americano all work well in place of the Campari, or use Byrrh instead of the vermouth.

APÉRITIFS AND LIQUEURS, GENERALLY

NEWLY ARRIVING EXPATS IN 1920s PARIS QUICKLY learned that, in Paris, *l'heure d'apéritif*—what Americans might vulgarly call "happy hour"—was an institution, if not a sacred ritual. And while "American bars" and cocktails continued to expand their influence, Parisians still relied on their faithful liqueurs, fortified wines, and other apéritifs at that magic hour of the day.

The venerable drinks writer G. Selmer Fougner, in his *New York Sun* column "Along the Wine Trail," observed that *l'heure d'apéritif* was "the most enjoyable moment of the day . . . when from a chair on the boulevard one may watch the world go by while sipping on one of the long, refreshing drinks in which Parisians delight."

Different writers, of course, had differing views on the local customs. In *Tropic of Cancer* you'll find Henry Miller's protagonist explaining, "You mustn't think I had a stomach like that when I came here. . . . That's from all the poison I was given to drink. . . . Those horrible *apéritifs* which the French are so crazy to drink." And in the *Toronto Star Weekly*, Ernest Hemingway informed readers back home that "apéritifs, or appetizers, are those tall, bright red or yellow drinks that are poured . . . by hurried waiters during the hour before lunch and the hour before dinner, when all Paris gathers at the cafes to poison themselves to a cheerful pre-eating glow," and that they all "have a basic taste like a brass doorknob, and go by such names as Amourette, Anis Delloso [*sic*], Amer Picon, Byrrh, Tomyysette and twenty others." Perhaps he eventually acquired a taste for them; he was only a lad of twenty-two when he wrote this.

In a comical scene from *The Sun Also Rises*, Hemingway's protagonist Jake Barnes learns that disdaining a local liqueur might cause some hurt feelings, but nothing that couldn't be fixed. After a big dinner in Bayonne, which included a bottle of Château Margaux (because, after all, "a bottle of wine was good company"), Jake considered a liqueur. "The waiter recommended a Basque liqueur called Izarra," explaining that it was "made of the flowers of the Pyrenees." To Jake, "it looked like hair-oil and smelled like Italian *strega*." Jake sent it back, and ordered a Vieux Marc (see page 18). When Jake sensed he'd hurt the waiter's feelings, he "overtipped him. That made him happy. It felt comfortable to be in a country where it is so simple to make people happy. You can never tell whether a Spanish waiter will thank you. Everything is on such a clear financial basis in France. It is the simplest country to live in."

Sometimes the choices could be daunting. In *Tender Is the Night*, F. Scott Fitzgerald's protagonist Dick Diver stared in silence "at a shelf that held the humbler poisons of France—bottles of Otard, Rhum St. James, Marie Brizzard [*sic*], Punch Orangeade, André Fernet Blanco, Cherry Rochet [*sic*], and Armagnac." In *The Sun Also Rises*, Robert Cohn and Jake Barnes surveyed the wide range of offerings. "Cohn looked at the bottles in bins around the wall. 'This is a good place,' he said. 'There's a lot of liquor,'" Jake agreed. Stateside papers observed that a newcomer to Paris "looks wistfully at some of these appetizing mixtures, and wishes he knew what to ask for in order to get them," while cheekily cautioning readers to take it easy; after all, "a couple of Picon-citron" or "mandarins-curaçoa" are likely to be followed by a demoralizing sense of irresponsibility.

While an entire book could be written on the many varieties, I'll focus on the more popular ones. Some are discussed separately, notably Pernod, Anis Del Oso, Amer Picon, crème de cassis, Suze, Campari, and kirschwasser (which also went by "kirsch," for short).* In 1932, there was the launch of Ricard pastis, which is an anise with

---

* See "Kirschwasser" (page 173).

licorice root added (note: a true anise does not contain licorice, per se, it only *tastes* like licorice due to the star anise). Among the other notable "appetizers," then and now, are Dubonnet, St Raphaël, Byrrh (pronounced "beer"), L.N. Mattei Cap Corse, Cocchi Americano, and Kina Lillet (now Lillet Blanc). These are wine-based beverages with the bark from the cinchona tree (the source of quinine), and other flavorings added, known as quinquina.

Several orange liqueurs were also popular, from Cointreau and Grand Marnier to a variety of brands of orange curaçao, as well as mandarin. In John Dos Passos's 1932 novel, *Nineteen Nineteen*, he writes: "They were drinking little glasses of Cointreau. . . . She kept pouring out more little glasses of Cointreau and Miss Felton seemed to be getting a little tipsy. . . . Eveline felt her own head swimming in the stuffy dark closedup [*sic*] little room."

"The Long, Refreshing Drinks in Which Parisians Delight"

Note that many of these apéritifs and liqueurs were frequently made into "long" or "tall" drinks, with the addition of juice, seltzer, or tonic water. What follows is a list of such drinks served at the cafés of Paris, many of which are still offered today. All may be served in a Collins or highball glass with ice.

Anis Del Oso and Grenadine: 1 ounce Anis Del Oso, ½ ounce grenadine, top with seltzer.

Byrrh and Cassis: 1 ounce Byrrh, ½ ounce crème de cassis, top with seltzer.

Cinzano and Cassis: 1 ounce Cinzano sweet vermouth, ½ ounce crème de cassis, top with seltzer.

Cinzano and Curaçao: 1 ounce Cinzano sweet vermouth, ½ ounce orange curaçao, top with seltzer.

Kirsch and Cassis: ½ ounce kirschwasser, 1 ounce crème de cassis, top with seltzer.

Kirsch and Grenadine: 1 ounce kirschwasser, ½ ounce crème de cassis, top with seltzer.

Picon and Cointreau: 1 ounce Amer Picon, ½ ounce Cointreau, top with seltzer.

Picon and Grenadine: 1 ounce Amer Picon, ½ ounce grenadine, top with seltzer.

St Raphaël and Citron: 1 ounce St Raphaël, ½ ounce fresh lemon juice, ½ ounce seltzer.

Suze and Cassis: 1 ounce Suze, ½ ounce crème de cassis, ½ ounce seltzer.

Vermouth and Curaçao: 1 ounce dry vermouth, ½ ounce orange curaçao, top with seltzer.

The fortified wines of nearby Italy, Portugal, and Spain were also quite popular, notably Sherry, Port, Marsala, and Madeira. "Fortified" means that you begin with wine, then add distilled wine (brandy) to make it higher proof. Amontillado is one of several varieties of Sherry, which is spelled *Xérès* in French and *Jerez* in Spanish.

Then you have the broad category of eau-de-vie, brandies distilled from fruit-based wines (other than grapes). It literally means "water of life." Gertrude Stein served framboise (raspberry) and mirabelle and quetsch (both made from plums) to her guests. In *A Moveable Feast*, Hemingway recalled that her salon was like a museum "except there was a big fireplace and it was warm and comfortable and they gave you . . . natural distilled liqueurs made from purple plums, yellow plums or wild raspberries . . . ," which "all tasted like the fruits they came from, converted into a controlled fire on your tongue that warmed you and loosened your tongue."

In prose from that era, a reference to *fine* is to Fine Champagne

Cognac. In *The Sun Also Rises*, Jake and Bill had dinner at Madame Lecomte's on the Île Saint Louis, and "after the coffee and a *fine* we got the bill, chalked up the same as ever on a slate . . ." In addition to Cognac and Armagnac* from France, you had Fundador, a Spanish style of brandy.

And then there's Amer Picon, a French apéritif bitter that is fairly impossible to find in America and, like other iconic brands (Coca-Cola, Bacardi rum, Gordon's gin, and Kina Lillet, for example), isn't what it used to be. Torani Amer is often suggested as a substitute, but it's also elusive (and also not a true match). Other alternatives include Bigallet China-China, Amaro CioCiaro, or Ramazzotti (with the addition of orange bitters). There's also a concoction known as Amer Boudreau, devised by bartender Jamie Boudreau, made with Ramazzotti, orange bitters, and other ingredients.†

Another popular after-dinner spirit was marc or vieux marc (pronounced "marrh"), if from France, or grappa (if from Italy), the "vieux" implying that it's been aged in oak barrels. These are brandies distilled from pomace, the leftovers of the winemaking process, i.e., grape skins, pulp, seeds, and stems. They're an acquired taste, and can be harsh on the palate.

Kümmel is a sweet liqueur flavored with carraway seeds, fennel, and cumin. It is popular in Germany and the Alps. Schnapps, depending on its origin, could be either a spirit distilled from fruit or a sweet, syrupy liqueur flavored with herbs or fruit (such as peppermint or peach).

Then as now, there are many other products to be experienced, with new offerings coming on the market and old brands being revived. Under today's apéritif heavens, the situation is excellent.

---

* Cognac and Armagnac are both grape brandies made from specific regions of France.

† Complete recipe found here: https://spiritsandcocktails.wordpress.com/2007/09/09/amer-picon.

THE ROLE OF THE
CAFÉ AND BISTRO

Like no other city, the sidewalk cafés of Paris are an essential part of the city, part of its signature. Robert Forrest Wilson observed, "There is nothing the stranger notices sooner on his first visit to the French capital than the part played by Paris's sidewalks . . ." The café and bistro served a multitude of roles, for Parisians and expats alike.

In his 1928 classic, *Paris Salons, Cafés, Studios,* Sisley Huddleston observed, "The café in France, more than in any other country, is the forcing ground of art and literature. . . . It has brought together many men who, exchanging their ideas in this public drawing-room, and have stimulated each other." Ralph Waldo Emerson noted that the "supreme merit ⟨of Paris⟩ is that it is the city of conversation in cafés."

Certain cafés had their own particular clientele. In his 1937 book, *The Spirit of Paris,* Paul Cohen-Portheim noted that "the cafés of the Latin Quarter and Montparnasse, and many small ones elsewhere, have a regular circle of patrons from the neighborhood. Most of the social intercourse of the Montparnasse artists takes place in the cafés . . ." To the Americans of Montparnasse, the Café du Dôme served as the "front porch, reception hall, parlor and sitting-room in one. It is home." Stephen Longstreet noted, "Individuals and groups adopted particular cafés. At the Rotonde, the Spaniards held an afternoon *peña* or discussion group, chaired by the day's fashionable intellectual. Germans and English prefer the Café du Dôme. . . . The Sélect stayed open all night, a magnet for drunks, whores and assorted mysteries." Henry Miller was said to sit for hours at the Dôme, his consumption of Cognac and coffees marked by the stack of saucers at his elbow.

You'll often see reference to saucers in both biographies and prose. In Paris, drinks were served on a saucer, with the price of the drink displayed on the bottom. A stack of saucers meant that person had had quite a few. On one visit to Paris, H. L. Mencken bragged his pile of saucers was so tall they "had to be secured with guy ropes." In his 1935 novel, *Of Time and the River*, Thomas Wolfe had one of his characters "sitting at a table on the terrace, and already very gay. Starwick would have a stack of saucers racked up before him on the table."

Four artists having drinks at the Café du Dôme, circa 1910.
Note the stack of saucers! LEFT TO RIGHT: *Wilhelm Uhde, Walter Bondy,*
Rudolf Levy, and Jules Pascin. Photo appeared in Billy Klüver and
Julie Martin, *Kiki's Paris: Artists and Lovers, 1900–1930*
(New York: Harry N. Abrams, Inc, 1988).

Meanwhile, the Café des Deux Magots, on the boulevard Saint-Germain, "was something like neutral ground, a vague no man's land between opposing camps and between the Right Bank and the Left, being a favorite resort of journalists and of Sorbonne professors . . . It was to the Deux Magots that one took a new acquaintance when uncertain as to just how to place him. The atmosphere as a rule was a tranquil one, a relief to the Montparnassians who wanted to get away from it all. Of an afternoon one might find Hemingway there, or Ezra Pound . . . and . . . Ford Madox Ford would likely be seated at one of the tables, surrounded by a carefully chosen audience of two or three."

Morley Callaghan recalled that the three neighboring cafés, Brasserie Lipp, Café de Flore, and Deux Magots, were "a focal point, the real Paris for illustrious intellectuals . . . André Gide might be having dinner at the Deux Magots. Picasso often passed on the street." Callaghan referred to the Deux Magots as "a center of International Paris life." All three cafés remain open today.

Janet Flanner, who wrote Paris-themed stories for the *New Yorker* under the pen name "Genêt," recalled that "the Surrealists had their own club table facing the door of the Deux Magots, from which vantage point a seated Surrealist could conveniently insult any new-comer with whom he happened to be feuding, or discuss his plan to horsewhip an editor of some belligerent anti-Surrealist newspaper for having mentioned his name or, worse, for having failed to men-tion it." Hemingway and Flanner had their own special table in the back, for their own deep conversations. Meanwhile, the "Café de Flore serves as a drugstore for pretty upstate girls in unbecoming blue denim pants and their Middle Western dates, most of whom are growing hasty Beaux-Arts beards."

The café also served as a place to write. Hemingway favored "a pleasant café, warm and clean and friendly" on the Place Saint-Michel, or else the Closerie des Lilas, his "home café," where it "was warm inside in the winter and in the spring and fall it was very fine outside with the tables under the shade of the trees." Here, he could escape the "people from the Dôme and the Rotonde," and "no one was on exhibition."

Speaking of warmth in the winter, let's not forget that sometimes it simply made sense to spend a cold day at a warm café rather than heat one's flat. A Vermouth Cassis cost only six cents, and the "pur-chase of two or more drinks" entitled one to stay "as long as one liked. It seemed extravagant, but one had to remember, in winter, that a bucket of coal to heat one's garret would cost just as much—and at the café one had the drinks besides. So it really was an economy, besides being gayer."

Callaghan recalled that on the typical café terrace, "a whole life went on there, a life in the open, the talented and the useless, living in each other's pockets, living on each other's dreams . . ." Further, one could move from one café to the next. "When we had had our fill of the faces and the snatches of conversation at the Coupole, we strolled along the boulevard as far as the Closerie des Lilas. How lovely the lighted tables spread out under the chestnut trees looked that April night; a little oasis of conviviality."

For essayist and novelist Anaïs Nin, the café offered a place for companionship. "The home and the studio were private. . . . But one was sure never to be lonely, for in the evening after work, one could always walk into certain cafés and find friends gathered there." This sentiment echoes through Hemingway's short story "A Clean, Well-Lighted Place." It explored the importance of the café, for "those who like to stay late" since "a clean, well-lighted café was a very different thing." Nin also concluded that "the hours I have spent in cafés are the only ones I call living, apart from writing."

The cafés and bistros of Paris weren't just for the expats, of course, and there was an egalitarian nature to them. "The entire population of Paris, it seems, sits down to drink and chatter. . . . The Paris laboring man, the plasterer, and the painter, in his white jumpers and wooden shoes, comes into the Bistro and stands, in perfect equality, alongside the French business man or Advocate, and sips his glass of wine. . . . No snobbishness in Paris; no irritability, no airs."

BACARDI COCKTAIL

HARRY'S NEW YORK BAR RECIPE

1½ ounces Bacardi rum
¾ ounce London dry gin
½ ounce fresh lime juice
1 teaspoon grenadine

Shake well with ice, then strain into a chilled cocktail glass.

Recipe from Barflies and Cocktails *(1927).*

RITZ BAR RECIPE

2 ounces Bacardi rum
1 teaspoon dry vermouth
¼ ounce fresh lemon juice
½ teaspoon grenadine

Shake well with ice, then strain into a chilled cocktail glass.

Recipe from The Artistry of Mixing Drinks *(1936).*

THE BACARDI COCKTAIL IS ONE OF THE ALL-TIME CLASSICS, first appearing in Jacques Straub's 1914 book, *Drinks*. It's basically a Daiquiri but with grenadine in place of (or supplementing) the simple syrup/sugar. Although the recipe is fairly settled nowadays, you did see some variety earlier on. In *Jack's Manual* (1916), it also

Cover of Mud Puddle's reproduction of Barflies and Cocktails. IMAGE COURTESY OF MUD PUDDLE INC. AND COCKTAILKINGDOM.COM.

includes both sweet and dry vermouth. Of course, Paris being Paris, they put their own stamp on the Bacardi. Here's how:

At Harry's New York Bar, they added a bit of gin, whereas at the Ritz, Frank Meier had dry vermouth in his Bacardi Cocktail. This latter approach is not uncommon—you'll find any number of classic cocktails using rum and dry vermouth, witness the immortal Presidente from Cuba. And in *Manual de Cantinero* (1925), you'll find a Cuban Cocktail, made with Bacardi, lemon, bitters, and dry vermouth. Try either of the Bacardi Cocktail recipes, and transplant yourself to Harry's or the Ritz, whichever one you fancy.

Zelda Fitzgerald was a Bacardi fan. F. Scott wasn't the only writer in the family, as Zelda published several short stories and the 1932 novel *Save Me the Waltz*. Zelda featured the Bacardi in her 1929 story,

"The Original Follies Girl." She described the protagonist: "I saw her not long ago under the trees in the Champs-Élysées. She looked like a daffodil. She was taking a yellow linen sports thing for an airing and she reeked of lemony perfume and Bacardi cocktails."

And you'll find more than a few references to the Bacardi in Harry Crosby's journal, where he told of drinking "Baccardi [*sic*] cocktails with brown sugar," or having a "Baccardi [*sic*] cocktail" at the Ritz Bar. Ever the poet, Harry glumly wrote that his wife, Caresse, was leaving Paris for New York, "and it is a gray day and rain is about to fall and it gets dark very early and I drink a rose-gold Baccardi [*sic*] cocktail (always the desire to pray when drinking cocktails)."

☞ **TASTING NOTE:** The addition of gin in Harry's offering makes for a drier cocktail, and the Ritz's use of vermouth adds complexity and bouquet.

THE BAILEY

1½ – 2 ounces London dry gin
½ ounce fresh grapefruit juice
½ ounce fresh lime juice
1 teaspoon simple syrup (optional)
2 sprigs of mint

"The mint should be put in the shaker first. It should be torn up by hand as it steeps better. The gin should be added then and allowed to stand a minute or two. Then add the grapefruit juice and then the lime juice. Stir vigorously with ice and do not allow to dilute too much, but serve very cold, with a sprig of mint in each glass."

Strain contents of shaker into a chilled cocktail or wineglass, garnish with the second mint sprig.

Recipe from a letter Gerald Murphy wrote to Alexander Woollcott.

THIS IS ONE OF TWO GERALD MURPHY ORIGINALS found herein, along with the Juice of a Few Flowers (page 120). Gerald and his wife, Sara, were wealthy Americans who moved to Paris in 1921. They joined a horde of other Yanks who'd decided that the United States was becoming too puritanical and stifling. As Gerald explained, they left partly because "there was something depressing … about a country that could pass the Eighteenth Amendment. The country was tightening up and it was so unbecoming. . . . It was, I suppose, the tone of life in America that we all found so uncongenial."

They had an apartment in Paris but summered in Cap d'Antibes. In fact, they are largely credited with "inventing" the Riviera's summer season. Vacationers typically went to more northerly resorts such as Deauville, but when the Murphys convinced the owner of the Hôtel du Cap-Eden-Roc to remain open for the summer of 1923, it became a lasting tradition. Not many foreigners could have pulled this off, but "the French found them chic." Perhaps it helped that Pablo Picasso was with them that summer.

The French weren't alone in being captivated by the Murphys. In his 1934 novel, *Tender Is the Night*, F. Scott Fitzgerald not only based the two main characters (Dick and Nicole Diver) on Gerald and Sara (and dedicated the book to them), he also highlighted their Riviera "invention." When Rosemary, a young American actress, meets the Divers, Rosemary asks Nicole, "Do you like it here—this place?" Before she can answer, Abe North (said to have been based on writer Ring Lardner) cuts in: "They have to like it. They invented it." The Murphys purchased a dilapidated old farm on a hillside overlooking the Mediterranean, restored it, and named it Villa America. Both here and in Paris, the Murphys became the focal point of a large circle, which included F. Scott and Zelda Fitzgerald, Ernest and Hadley (and later Pauline) Hemingway, Picasso, Archibald and Ada MacLeish, Cole Porter, John Dos Passos, Dorothy Parker, Robert Benchley, Fernand Léger, Jean Cocteau, Philip Barry, Igor Stravinsky, Rudolph Valentino, the French actress Mistinguett, and many others.

Donald Ogden Stewart, who won the Oscar for his screenplay adaptation of Philip Barry's play *The Philadelphia Story*, described the Murphys, saying, "They were both rich; he was handsome; she was beautiful; they had three golden children. They loved each other, they enjoyed their own company, and they had the gift of making life enchantingly pleasurable for those who were fortunate enough to be their friends."

Their influence on the world of art and literature was profound. At Yale, Gerald encouraged Cole Porter to write songs for school plays. As noted, F. Scott Fitzgerald "borrowed" them in *Tender Is the Night*

Vintage ad. IMAGE COURTESY OF LUCAS BOLS AMSTERDAM.

(the first half, anyway; the characters would transform into F. Scott and Zelda as things went sour). And in any Picasso painting with a woman on the beach wearing pearls, that's Sara. She'd say her pearls needed the occasional sunshine.

The Murphys' parties were legendary, which Sara referred to as a "Dinner-Flowers-Gala," a term she borrowed from luxury ocean liners of the day. At Villa America, an evening began with cocktails on the terrace (never more than two), made by Gerald. It was said that "even the most mundane act—the way Gerald prepared a cocktail . . . was somehow transformed into a memorable event." That he would become so engrossed in fixing a drink caused Philip Barry to remark, "Gerald, you look as though you're saying Mass." According to son-in-law William Donnelly:

The Murphy cocktail hour was a unique production. As the hour approached, Sara would place on the bar small Steuben pitchers containing orange, lemon, and lime juice, always fresh. This man didn't mix drinks, he performed an office. He looked like a chemist or magician, measuring, mixing, holding up to the light, garnishing, and, finally, serving with a flourish. . . . . His opinion of drinking was that he loved drinking but disliked drunks. He had mixed a batch of drinks one evening. . . . As they watched the sunset from my terrace, Gerald remarked that "this drink has gone right to my head, which is just what I intended it to do."

☛ **TASTING NOTE:** The Bailey is a tart, refreshing drink. It resembles the classic Southside, said to have been favored by Chicago's Southside mob during Prohibition. For reasons unknown, it's also a staple in the Hamptons of Long Island, where, coincidentally, both Sara and Gerald lived their last days.

ANOTHER MEMORABLE
MURPHY SOIRÉE

While Gerald and Sara were known for lavish evenings at Villa America, at least one of their Paris fetes was legendary. In the summer of 1923, to celebrate the opening of Igor Stravinsky's ballet *Les Noces*, they hosted an after-party. They tried to rent the Cirque Médrano but were denied by a snooty manager. "The *Cirque Médrano* is not yet an American colony," he haughtily sniffed. So they held their soirée on a *péniche*, a converted barge located on the Seine, in front of the National Assembly.

Vintage postcard showing a péniche, *or barge, on the Seine.* FROM THE AUTHOR'S COLLECTION.

After cocktails on the canopied upper deck of the *péniche*, the guests drifted downstairs . . . all except Cocteau, whose horror of seasickness was so excruciating that he refused to come on board until the last Seine excursion boat, with its rolling wake, had gone by. The champagne dinner that followed was memorable, and so was the décor.

As the event was held on a Sunday, no fresh flowers were available, so Sara improvised by making a centerpiece on the banquet table fashioned from toys, dolls, and other sundries found at a Montparnasse bazaar. Picasso was enchanted by the collection and soon rearranged them into a creative display. The highlight of the evening came when Stravinsky took a running leap through the center of a huge laurel wreath. Cocteau eventually relaxed and "donned the captain's dress uniform and went from porthole to porthole, announcing, *'On coule!'*" ("We're sinking!")

While only about forty people attended, "the Murphys' *péniche* party has assumed over the years a sort of legendary aura, so that people who may or may not have been there give vivid . . . descriptions of the event. The . . . people who *were* there constituted a kind of summit meeting of the modern movement in Paris: Picasso, Darius Milhaud, Jean Cocteau, Ernest Ansermet (who conducted *Les Noces*), Germaine Tailleferre, Marcelle Meyer, Serge Diaghilev, Natalia Goncharova and ⟨Mikhail⟩ Larionov, Tristan Tzara, Blaise Cendrars, Cole Porter, and Scofield Thayer, the editor of the *Dial*." John Dos Passos, who attended many of the ballet's rehearsals (along with E. E. Cummings), somehow managed to miss it. "Nobody organized more amusing affairs. I always regretted missing the famous party they gave to *tout Paris* on a barge on the Seine."

THE BEE'S KNEES

2 ounces London dry gin
¹/₃ ounce fresh lemon juice
1 teaspoon honey

Shake well with ice, then strain into a chilled cocktail glass or coupe.

Recipe from The Artistry of Mixing Drinks *(1936).*

THE 1920s BROUGHT US A GREAT MANY THINGS, NOTABLY postwar prosperity, Prohibition, jazz, the flapper, and a few wacky additions to the popular lexicon. "Twenty-three skiddoo," "cat's pajamas," "daddyo," and "you're all wet" were flying from the lips of hep cats of the day. One such idiom was "the bee's knees." Rather than saying something stuffy like "I just think she's swell," you could really wow 'em with "She's the bee's knees!"

A 1929 story in the *New Orleans Item-Tribune* told of two American girls who'd been raised in Korea, and upon their return to the States they were bewildered by the new vernacular.

"My goodness," said Harriette to a curious newspaperman. "I nearly fell out of my seat on a train the other day when some person said that he'd tell the cockeyed world that some girl was the 'bee's knees,' whatever that is. Everywhere we find that girls aren't girls, but 'wrens,' 'mamas,' 'bims,' 'frails,' 'skirts,' 'babies,' 'gold diggers,' 'broads,' and a dozen other things." "Yessir," laughed Harriette, "this new Yankee chatter has me all haywire!"

Frank Meier (left) with his team of bartenders, at the Paris Ritz Bar.
PHOTOGRAPH COURTESY OF THE HOTEL RITZ PARIS.

This is one of the many classic drinks credited to Frank Meier, head bartender of the Paris Ritz Bar. The drink was an early instance of using honey as the sweetener (thus the origin of the name). In addition to Meier's book, you'll find it in the 1929 book *Cocktails de Paris* by Georges Gabriel Thenon.

☞ **TASTING NOTE:** Try fixing this for someone who says they don't like gin, and you'll likely have a convert. This is a delicious drink with the tartness of the lemon balanced by the honey. The trick is to shake it well and serve it very cold.

THE BLOODY MARY

1½ ounces vodka
4 ounces tomato juice
½ ounce fresh lemon (or lime) juice
3 dashes pepper sauce, such as Tabasco
3 dashes Worcestershire sauce
Other seasonings, to taste (such as celery salt,
cayenne, et cetera)
Garnish(es) of your choosing

Shake gently with ice, then transfer to a highball glass. Garnish with celery stalk, a pickled string bean or okra, or any other item of your choosing.

Recipe based on Ernest Hemingway's own formula.

THE BLOODY MARY HAS AT LEAST TWO CONNECTIONS with the City of Light. A longstanding story tells us that the Bloody Mary was invented at Harry's New York Bar in the early 1920s by Fernand "Pete" Petiot. His obituary noted that he was "experimenting with vodka drinks after having been introduced to the Russian spirit in 1920." His original formula was a fifty-fifty mixture of vodka and tomato juice. An American named Roy Barton suggested that Pete name the drink the Bucket of Blood, after a Chicago bar. The drink apparently never caught on in Paris, and by 1934, Pete had taken his talents, and his drink, to New York's St. Regis hotel. There, he changed the name to the Red Snapper, as the hotel found the drink's name to be a bit too, well . . . *bloody*.

This creation theory is backed by the presumed 1929 memoir of a man who used the pen name W. W. Windstaff. He was reportedly killed in 1931, and his memoirs were published by Stephen Longstreet in 1993 under the title *Lower Than Angels: A Memoir of War & Peace*. It's a coarse and often profane remembrance of 1920s Paris. Within its pages, Windstaff claimed that "Harry's New York Bar in Paris is the birthplace of the Bloody Mary and sidecar cocktail." While this seems pretty convincing, I'm a bit dubious. Why? First off, the earliest-known reference to the Bloody Mary by name occurred ten years later, in 1939. Further, the "memoir" has several other likely anachronisms, such as a claim that Hemingway made "a romance out of killing animals and fish, and dying." Such a blanket statement seems premature in 1929, before he'd been to Africa, written his treatise on bullfighting, or gained a reputation as a big-game hunter and fisherman. Nevertheless, Windstaff's "memoirs" are offered for your consideration.

Another Bloody Mary origin story concerns American entertainer George Jessel, who claimed to have first mixed vodka and tomato juice in Palm Beach as early as 1927. He said he mixed one up for his friend Mary Warburton, and when her drink spilled on her white dress, she blurted out, "Now you can call me Bloody Mary, George!"

When interviewed in *New Yorker* magazine in 1964, Pete Petiot said, "I initiated the Bloody Mary of today. . . . I cover the bottom of the shaker with four large dashes of salt, two dashes of black pepper, two dashes of cayenne pepper, and a layer of Worcestershire sauce; I then add a dash of lemon juice and some cracked ice, put in two ounces of vodka and two ounces of thick tomato juice, shake, strain, and pour."

The other Paris story concerns, of all people, Ernest Hemingway, who was quite fond of the Bloodys served at the Ritz Bar by bartender Bertin Azimont. In later years, Hemingway "adopted the bar as his Head Quarters and spent many hours there planning his strategies for the horse races at Auteuil . . . under the profound inspiration of Bertin's Bloody Marys." In fact, Azimont claimed that he invented the drink and named it after Hemingway's fourth wife, Mary. As the story goes, Hemingway wanted a drink that couldn't be detected on his breath, since his "bloody wife" Mary was hassling him about his drinking. Alas, this yarn doesn't match up with the facts, as Hemingway and Mary didn't wed until 1946, long after the drink was established. But it is, like so many others, a good story.

And so, the immortal Bloody Mary remains in that crowded category of drinks whose progeny is unknown. Was it invented at Harry's New York Bar? While I can't prove that it wasn't, it's important to note that the drink does not appear in either of owner Harry MacElhone's books, *Barflies and Cocktails* and *ABC of Mixing Cocktails*. But that could be because the drink never really took off at Harry's. Yet, as you'll soon learn, the influx of Russians to the city meant that the previously exotic spirit known as vodka was becoming popular in 1920s Paris. In fact, Smirnoff opened a distillery there in 1925, and you'll find any number of recipes using vodka in the French cocktail books of the day. So the question remains open for debate.

☞ **TASTING NOTE:** The Bloody Mary offers the opportunity to experiment, varying the amount of spice and heat (celery salt, pepper sauce, Worcestershire, et cetera), the level of tartness (more or less lemon), and innovative items for the garnish.

THE RUSSIANS ARE COMING! THE RUSSIANS ARE COMING!

I mentioned earlier that Pete Petiot was "experimenting with vodka drinks after having been introduced to the Russian spirit in 1920." How might the denizens of Paris have come to be exposed to, as Ezra Pound called them, "the Rooshians," not to mention their spirit of choice?

The Russian Revolution (1917) resulted in the downfall of Czar Nicholas II and the creation of a Soviet government, led by Vladimir Lenin, with the assistance of his lieutenant Leon Trotsky. Little-known fact: Lenin and Trotsky were regulars at the Café de la Rotonde prior to the revolution, where they'd "meet over a chess-board and plan to manipulate kings and nations as they manipulated their pawns and pieces."

The revolution resulted in the mass exodus of so-called white Russians, and many sought refuge in Paris. Almost overnight, the Rotonde went from a revolutionary incubator to a sanctuary for exiles, hopeful of a restoration of the *ancien régime*. Ernest Hemingway wrote a breezy piece on this phenomenon in the *Toronto Daily Star* in 1922, noting that the Rotonde was a gathering place for "Russians . . . drifting along in Paris in a childish sort of hopefulness that things will somehow be all right, which is all quite charming when you first encounter it and rather maddening after a few months. . . . But there is a great probability that nothing very wonderful nor unexpected will happen and then, eventually, like all the rest of the world, the Russians of Paris may have to go to work. It seems a pity, they are such a charming lot."

Indeed, the legendary clothing designer and *parfumier* Gabrielle "Coco" Chanel had her own dalliance with Russian nobility, a whirlwind affair with the exiled Grand Duke Dmitri Pavlovich in 1920. He was described as "a blond young fellow who is seldom seen on successive occasions with the same dinner partner." It seems their affair fizzled when he insisted their marriage be "morganatic," meaning if Russia's nobility were to be restored, neither she nor any resulting children would be royals. "Gabrielle objected to this and her romance . . . is a part of the history of things that might have been. Paris is a city of such tales."

Chanel blithely concluded, "Those Grand Dukes were all the same—they looked marvelous but there was nothing behind. . . . They were tall and handsome and splendid, but behind it all—nothing: just vodka and the void."

BŒUF SUR LE TOIT

1½ ounces London dry gin
¾ ounce plum liqueur
¾ ounce orange curaçao

Stir well with ice, then strain into a chilled cocktail glass.

Recipe from Cocktails de Paris *(1929).*

THIS WAS THE SIGNATURE DRINK OF A RESTAURANT AND nightclub known as Le Boeuf sur le Toit, which opened to great fanfare on January 10, 1922. The origin of the name is a bit complicated. French composer Darius Milhaud discovered a Brazilian folk song called "O Boi no Telhado," which means "the bull on the roof." Milhaud created a musical about a man who kept a menagerie in his attic apartment, including a bull calf. His neighbors complained, it went to court, and a judge ordered their removal. But by this time the calf had grown and was too large to remove. Milhaud's friend Jean Cocteau then created a farcical ballet, also using the same name.

At this time, in Montparnasse, there was a group of musicians known as Les Six, made up of Milhaud, Georges Auric, Louis Durey, Arthur Honegger, Francis Poulenc, and Germaine Tailleferre, with Cocteau as its informal leader. They would gather for dinner parties at Milhaud's apartment. A typical evening included "cocktails and hijinks, including occasional bicycle races around the dining-room table." They soon moved to a bar called Le Gaya, owned by Louis

A typical night at Le Boeuf sur le Toit, circa 1926.
PHOTOGRAPH COURTESY OF LE BOEUF SUR LE TOIT, PARIS.

Moysès. These gatherings attracted more and more people, including celebrities such as Pablo Picasso, Serge Diaghilev, Arthur Rubinstein, and Maurice Chevalier, and they outgrew Le Gaya. Moysès, sensing an opportunity, found a new venue, at 28 rue Boissy d'Anglas, and he named his new restaurant and cabaret Le Boeuf sur le Toit. In the words of painter Jean Hugo, Le Boeuf became "the crossroads of destinies, the cradle of love-affairs, the home of discords, the navel of Paris."

The walls were covered by the works of Man Ray, Picasso, Cocteau, Francis Picabia, and other renowned artists. Cocteau noted that "the Boeuf was not a bar at all, but a kind of club, the meeting place of all the best people in Paris, from all spheres of life . . . the loveliest women, poets, musicians, businessmen, publishers—everybody met everybody at the Boeuf." From his deathbed in 1922, the great novelist Marcel Proust reportedly said, "If I could only be well enough to go once to the cinema, and to Le Boeuf sur le Toit."

According to Picasso biographer John Richardson, "Men were expected to wear dinner jackets, women to dress up in Chanel, Lanvin, or Vionnet. Overnight it became the headquarters of what would soon be known as café society, a place where high and low, *gens chic* and *gens louche*, could mingle with the leading lights of the avant-garde."

One Paris guidebook noted that it had "a real American jazz band that plays incessantly. One of the jolliest groups in up-town Paris. You dance and dine and make frequent trips to the bar. Good food and interesting boys and girls. Very few French. The piano pounder here gets all the new stuff, red hot from Broadway." A year after its opening, a young reporter named Ernest Hemingway reviewed in the *Toronto Daily Star*:

> Where is the really gay Paris nightlife we hear so much about? Where are the young people who never go to bed at night? . . . They are probably packed into a little place around the corner from the Hotel Crillon in the staidest, most respectable, un-Bohemian quarter of Paris. In the Rue Boissy d'Anglas is the café of the Boeuf sur le Toit . . . , Jean Cocteau's bar and dancing,* where everyone in Paris who believes that the true way to burn the candle is by igniting it at both ends goes. By eleven o'clock the Boeuf is so crowded that there is no more room to dance. But all the world is there.

Le Boeuf's runaway success caused some issues with its neighbors, causing it to move. It's now at 34 rue du Colisée, its fifth location. As a final note, Le Boeuf's namesake drink, created by the bar's manager Maurice, won the prestigious Coupe d'Honneur au Championnat des Barmen Professionels staged in Paris on February 2, 1929.

---

* In 1920s Paris, a "dancing" was a supper club.

☛ **TASTING NOTE:** You might not immediately love this drink, but give it a few sips. The softness of the plum marries well with the slight sweetness of the orange curaçao, offering a delicious counterpoint to the gin. Trimbach makes a fine mirabelle plum liqueur, or you might try the delicious Averell Damson Gin Liqueur. For the triple sec, go with Cointreau or Pierre Ferrand Dry Curaçao.

BØULEVARDIER

> **1 ounce Bourbon**
> **1 ounce sweet vermouth**
> **1 ounce Campari**
> **Maraschino cherry, for garnish**
>
> ---
>
> Stir all ingredients well with ice in a mixing glass, then strain into a rocks glass containing fresh ice. Garnish with a maraschino cherry.
>
> *Recipe from* Barflies and Cocktails *(1927).*

THE BOULEVARDIER IS OFTEN THOUGHT OF AS A NEGRONI, but with Bourbon in place of the gin. To me, the drink is a complex three-part cocktail that combines the stories of three pretty interesting gents who lived in 1920s Paris: Erskine Gwynne, Arthur Moss, and Jed Kiley.

The Boulevardier debuted in the "Cocktails Round Town" portion of Harry MacElhone's *Barflies and Cocktails*, a collection assembled by Harry's sidekick, Moss. Many of these drinks are forgettable, if not downright silly, but some are memorable, notably the Boulevardier, My Old Pal (page 146), and Pierre Loving's Pet Punch (page 156).

The Boulevardier entry reads: "Now is the time for all good Barflies to come to the aid of the party, since Erskinne [*sic*] Gwynne crashed in with his Boulevardier Cocktail: 1/3 Campari, 1/3 Italian vermouth, 1/3 Bourbon whisky."*

---

* For more about the "Barflies," see I.B.F. Pick-Me-Up (page 102).

So who were these three fellows, and where did the name Boulevardier come from? In 1927, Gwynne, Kiley, and Moss (along with Florence Gilliam) founded a magazine called *The Boulevardier*. It "was the expensive creation of a 'continental socialite' and member of the Vanderbilt family named Erskine Gwynne. Using the *New Yorker* as a model, Gwynne hoped his venture would appeal to the wealthy Anglo-American colony in Paris. . . . *The Boulevardier* attracted a few American and English writers, among them Ernest Hemingway, Noël Coward, Michael Arlen, and Louis Bromfield." Unfortunately, what worked in New York didn't work in Paris. "Gossipy stories, articles about horse racing, golf and yachting, and Gwynne's spicy and sometimes malicious column 'Ritz Alley' substantially outweighed the magazine's artistic offerings, and four years after he started it Gwynne brought *The Boulevardier* to a close."

It seems F. Scott Fitzgerald wasn't a fan of its gossip column, judging by his short story "News of Paris—Fifteen Years Ago":

> "I'll walk on the other side of the street," he said, "and then we'll meet at the door."
>
> "No, we oughtn't even to sit together. I'm a countess—laugh it off but anything I do will be in that damn 'Boulevardier.'"

Cofounder Kiley was quite the raconteur and man-about-town in 1920s Paris. He owned several nightclubs, notably Kiley's, which "offered dancing from midnight to breakfast, drawing capacity crowds every night. So popular was his place that the *Paris Herald Tribune*, widely read by Americans, regularly listed Kiley's as one of the best bars in Paris." According to legend, American jazz made its Paris debut at one of Kiley's clubs, in the form of a band called the White Lyres, made up of World War I vets.

Another cofounder was Moss, "a keen young man with an incisive cleverness which he works into the paragraphs of his column *Over the River. . . .* No reporter ever had an easier beat—nothing to do but sit on the Dôme terrace and let the tidings come to you." Perhaps it wasn't always so easy for Moss, such as that day he had a run-in with one of his writers.

Vintage Byrrh ad, depicting a Paris café during winter. Note the charcoal brazier on the right and the soda siphon on the table, as well as the puckish newsboy, stealing a sip of Byrrh. FROM THE AUTHOR'S COLLECTION.

It seems that a young buck named Hemingway submitted an essay titled "The Real Spaniard," an obscenity-laced parody of Bromfield. According to Kiley, "Gwynne read it, hit the ceiling, and grabbed a big blue pencil. 'Where does he write, on restroom walls?' he roared." When Hemingway found out his piece had been edited, he also hit the ceiling. He told Moss, who was five foot one: "If I were your size I'd knock your block off." Moss courageously replied, "If I were your size maybe I'd knock your block off." Hemingway suddenly lost his anger, smiled, and said: "Maybe you would. Let's have a drink." Maybe that drink was a Boulevardier. Isn't it pretty to think so?

As a final note, I recommend another Boulevardier Cocktail made in Paris at this time, the recipe coming from the 1929 book *Cocktails de Paris*. Here's how:

1 ounce Dubonnet
1 ounce St Raphaël
½ ounce Campari
½ ounce Courvoisier Cognac

Combine all ingredients in an ice-filled rocks glass. Stir well.

Invented by Robert Du Viel, it is said to have won the Grand Prix at the Championship of Barmen held in Paris on February 2, 1929. This one is interesting in that it has two different quinquina wines (Dubonnet and St Raphaël)* as its base. But don't expect this drink to taste as it would have in the 1920s. St Raphaël is difficult to find in the United States, and both brands have changed their formulas since the 1920s. Further, Dubonnet in France is quite different from what you can get in the States. I've made this drink with another quinquina (Byrrh) taking both their places and was very happy with the result.

☛ **TASTING NOTE:** Both of these Boulevardier variations, along with the Negroni and My Old Pal, show the versatility of the three-part Americano formula. Here, the Bourbon, vermouth, and Campari are made for one another; the trick is to stir it well with ice, then strain it into a glass with fresh ice; to simply "build" it in the glass might not make it cold enough. Lemon or orange peel are good garnish options. Dolin Rouge and Martini both make solid, affordable sweet vermouths, or try Miró or any of the other delicious bargains from Spain. If you're splurging, Carpano Antica Formula is sublime.

* See the discussion of quinquina wines within the Americano chapter (page 11).

BRANDY WITH CHERRIES

> **3 ounces brandy or Cognac**
> **4 cocktail cherries (such as Amarena Fabbri or Luxardo)**
> **Dash of absinthe**
>
> ---
>
> The drink is served neat, but you might want to add a lump of ice.

ONE OF THE FAVORITE HAUNTS OF MONTMARTRE WAS (and still is) quite different from its typical clubs and cabarets,* a "broken down shanty" known as Au Lapin Agile. It's described as "the oldest, oddest, rickety-est, little old building you ever saw," and "the most genuine and honest of the real Bohemian resorts of Paris . . . not tough, but rough, the old style natural, not dolled up for tourists in the slightest." Lapin Agile sits perched on what's known as La Butte, at 22 rue des Saules, a steep, winding and "tiny crooked street."

It's one of Paris's oldest entertainment venues, dating back to at least 1860. Lapin Agile literally means "the lively rabbit"; this goes back to artist André Gill, who painted a sign featuring a rabbit jumping out of a saucepan, circa 1870. Locals got to referring to the place as Le Lapin à Gill, and the latter part of the name blurred into "agile," which makes sense, too.

---

* See the chapter Champagne (page 69).

*Postcard of Le Lapin à Gill, a.k.a. Au Lapin Agile, circa 1872. To the right
of the upstairs window you can see André Gill's iconic painting of the rabbit
escaping a saucepan, with a bottle of wine, no less! That's one agile rabbit.*
FROM THE AUTHOR'S COLLECTION.

While it's a "cabaret," it's not what that term suggests—there's no
orchestra and long line of showgirls doing a risqué cancan. It has
more of a Greenwich Village coffeehouse, rustic inn, or Preservation
Hall vibe to it. It was a hangout for bohemians and celebrities
alike, notably Pablo Picasso, Amedeo Modigliani, Guillaume Apol-
linaire, Maurice Utrillo, Ernest Hemingway, Henry Miller, Charlie
Chaplin, Eleanor Roosevelt, Edward G. Robinson, Robert Mitchum,
Sir Laurence Olivier, Vivien Leigh, Paul Newman, Joanne Wood-
ward, Lauren Bacall, the list goes on.

The house drink, then and now, was simply brandy with a handful
of brandied cherries in the glass, served neat (though you may add a
lump of ice, as you like). The current owners have suggested to me
that the 1920s recipe also contained a "secret" dash of absinthe. The
1927 guide *Paris with the Lid Lifted* described a typical evening:

A low red light shines through the dirty window pane. You wonder, "What is this place?" The home of a beggar, perhaps. But no—a surprise awaits you. You enter and find a large center room filled with laughing, chanting, happy people. An old man is here, with a long white beard and a red Santa Claus cap. He is singing to them. It is wonderful. You drop on an old bench at an old table; a saucy girl brings you a glass of brandied cherries; the old man stops; the company applauds gleefully; a woman comes in and recites; a guitarist twangs; a harpist strums; another sings jolly old songs in which everyone joins—all in French; and your mouth flies open, and you listen and look on in amazement that anything could be so absolutely and utterly naïve, charming and lovely.

In 1905, Picasso gave his painting *At the Lapin Agile* to the cabaret, depicting himself dressed as a harlequin, and the owner, Frédé Gérard, playing the guitar. Frédé sold it for $20 in 1912. In 1989, it was sold at a Sotheby's auction for $41 million.

☛ **TASTING NOTE:** This simple little drink might just be what gets you to like brandy. The cherries offer a nice note of sweetness to the subtle grape of the spirit. Pierre Ferrand Ambre works well here.

BRANDY AND SODA / FINE À L'EAU

---

2 ounces brandy (or Cognac if making a *Fine à l'Eau*)
4 ounces seltzer water

Combine ingredients in a Collins glass filled with ice. Stir and serve.

THE TWO NAMES APPLY TO BASICALLY THE SAME DRINK; a *Fine à l'Eau* (translated as "Cognac and water") is made with Cognac, whereas a brandy and soda uses any grape brandy. The term *"fine"* is short for *Grande Fine Champagne*, meaning it's a blend of Grande Champagne and Petite Champagne Cognac. By either name, this drink was very popular in 1920s Paris, and you find many mentions in literature and biographies of the day.

As stated in the Rhum Saint-James chapter (page 165), Parisians were very fond of their French products, notably Armagnac and Cognac. And, as the American and British expats were keen to do as the locals did, they became brandy devotees. For example, in his 1929 novel, *A Farewell to Arms*, you find Ernest Hemingway's protagonist Frederic Henry finding solace in brandy as he and his lover Catherine escape from war-torn Italy into neutral Switzerland by rowboat. "I opened the bag and ate a couple of sandwiches and took a drink of the brandy. It made everything much better and I took another drink."

That's not to say that the practice was universally accepted; witness this bit of conversation between English novelist and publisher

Ford Madox Ford, playing the would-be mentor to the young Hemingway:

> "What are you drinking brandy for?" Ford asked me. "Don't you know it's fatal for a young writer to start drinking brandy?"
> "I don't drink it very often," I said.

A scene from Hemingway's *The Sun Also Rises* tells of an evening spent by Jake Barnes and friends, including his star-crossed lover, Brett Ashley. They've gone to a *bal musette*, an informal dance hall, rented by a character named Braddocks (based on Ford Madox Ford). Jake ordered a *Fine à l'Eau*, and finds himself talking to an insufferable young writer named Robert Prentiss (based on Glenway Wescott). Jake "was a little drunk. Not drunk in any positive sense but just enough to be careless." Fed up with Prentiss, Jake walks off. Mrs. Braddocks chides him. "Don't be cross with Robert," she said. "He's still only a child, you know." Jake replies, "I wasn't cross, I just thought perhaps I was going to throw up." Just then, Brett walked up:

> "Hello, you chaps."
> "Hello, Brett," I said. "Why aren't you tight?"
> "Never going to get tight any more. I say, give a chap a brandy and soda."

The brandy and soda / *Fine à l'Eau* appears throughout *The Sun Also Rises*, with Jake or Brett "getting brandy and soda and glasses," or reaching for the siphon (the seltzer water dispenser), to make a short one at home. The drink was also popular with the newspapermen of the day, notably Sparrow Robertson.* Ring Lardner told of a time when "a bunch of the boys at Harry's New York Bar in Paris held a lottery on the Sparrow's age." When it came time to determine the winner, they asked Sparrow how old he was.

> "Is there much money bet?" he asked.
> "Plenty," the boys assured him.

---

* See also My Old Pal (page 146).

"Well," said the Sparrow, swayed by the sporting nature of the emergency, "the highest one is the winner."

And he darted off in embarrassment to get his next Fine a l'Eau in another bar.

☞ **TASTING NOTE:** Brandy and Cognac are an acquired taste. While many enthusiasts enjoy theirs "neat" (no ice), think of this drink as an introduction, with the water and ice taking some of the edge off the spirit and opening it up. Sparkling water further helps to animate the brandy, which Hemingway described in his novel *The Garden of Eden*: "The cold Perrier had made the heavy brandy alive."

THE BALS MUSETTES

While there was certainly plenty of music and dancing at the clubs "up on the hill" of Montmartre, the bal musettes were where folks gathered for less formal fun. These were simple affairs; while the nightclubs were more glitz and glam, the bals had more of a local-dive vibe to them. As was described in a popular guidebook of the day, "Anyone wishing to see the French workingman at his pleasurable best can do no better than to visit a *bal musette*." Hemingway described the typical bal as a "little smoky room," where you might "dance to the music of a man with an accordion who keeps time with the stamping of his boots. . . . The people that go to the Bal Musette do not need to have the artificial stimulant of the jazz band to force them to dance. They dance for the fun of it."

Ernest and Hadley Hemingway's first address was a fourth-floor walk-up at 74 rue du Cardinal Lemoine. The ground floor was occupied by the Bal du Printemps. They "resented its noise, but danced there" often. Ford Madox Ford often rented out this bal for his weekend parties.

Also notable was the Bal de la Montagne Sainte-Geneviève, which Hemingway memorialized in *The Sun Also Rises* (while recycling his *Toronto Daily Star* piece):

> The dancing-club was a *bal musette* in the Rue de la Montagne Sainte Geneviève. Five nights a week the working people of the Pantheon quarter danced there. . . . The proprietor got up on a high stool beside the dancing-floor and began to play the accordion. He had a string of bells around one of his ankles and beat time with his foot as he played. Every one danced. It was hot and we came off the floor perspiring.
>
> "My God," Georgette said. "What a box to sweat in!"

Not all the musicians at Paris's bal musettes were amateurs. In fact, the great jazz musician Django Reinhardt got his start at the very same Bal de la Montagne Sainte-Geneviève.

BRANDY COCKTAIL

2 ounces Cognac or brandy
$^1/_3$ ounce simple syrup
2 dashes Angostura aromatic bitters
Lemon peel, for garnish

Stir all ingredients well in a mixing glass with ice, then strain into a chilled cocktail glass. Garnish with a lemon peel.

Recipe from Barflies and Cocktails *(1927).*

YOU MIGHT SAY THIS IS THE ORIGINAL COCKTAIL, AND you might be right. This simple drink is the embodiment of the now-famous 1806 definition of the word "cock-tail" that appeared in the Hudson, New York, newspaper *Balance, and Columbian Repository*: "spirits of any kind, sugar, water and bitters." Whether its base was brandy, gin, rum, or whiskey, it represented the state-of-the-art in cocktails for much of the nineteenth century. So when you drink this one, you're drinking an original.

Author George Orwell moved to Paris in the spring of 1928 and stayed nearly two years. His initial attempts at writing was a story of one rejection after another, which inspired his first published novel, *Down and Out in Paris and London* (1933). The book "does not chronicle a novelist's struggle to support his writing, but rather recounts the adventures of an author for whom the struggle seems to be its own end. Orwell merely wants edible food, a good night's sleep, and a roof above his head . . ."

Along with Ernest Hemingway's *A Moveable Feast*, it's yet another saga of the hungry, struggling young writer in Paris. While Hemingway tended to romanticize his situation ("but this is how Paris was in the early days when we were very poor and very happy"), Orwell had a different perspective: "It is a feeling of relief, almost of pleasure, at knowing yourself at last genuinely down and out. You have talked so often of going to the dogs—and well, here are the dogs, and you have reached them, and you can stand it. It takes off a lot of anxiety." He further reasoned, "Six francs is a shilling, and you can live on a shilling a day in Paris if you know how. But it is a complicated business."

In one scene, Orwell described the "stroke of luck" that befell the protagonist. As in his real life, he works as a *plongeur* (only the French could give the term "dishwasher" such panache). One evening an American customer called for him at table, ordering twenty-four Brandy Cocktails.

> I brought them all together on a tray, in twenty-four glasses. "Now, *garcon*,'" said the customer (he was drunk), "'I'll drink twelve and you'll drink twelve, and if you can walk to the door afterwards you get a hundred francs." I walked to the door, and he gave me a hundred francs. And every night for six days he did the same thing; twelve brandy cocktails, then a hundred francs. A few months later I heard he had been extradited by the American Government—embezzlement. There is something fine, do you not think, about these Americans?

☛ **TASTING NOTE:** This is another excellent introduction to brandy (or Cognac, Armagnac, or other expression). The sugar, bitters, the zest of the lemon peel, and the dilution from the ice soften the spirit. Pierre Ferrand's 1840 Cognac is perfect in this one.

AMERICANS INVADE PARIS,
WITH PLENTY OF CASH

World War I ended on November 11, 1918. For reasons that are more fully explained elsewhere in this book (see "Why Paris?" on page xiv), the City of Light became the place to be. And there was one other very compelling reason why Americans flocked to Paris: *it was damned cheap!*

It's not so much that the cost of living was low, necessarily; in fact, postwar France was in the grips of inflation. But that inflation led to a devaluation of the currency, resulting in a very favorable exchange rate. So while Hemingway liked to play up the whole "Hadley and I were very poor and very happy" line, between her small trust fund and his *Toronto Daily Star* salary, they were able to live somewhat comfortably, if modestly, and use the money they saved to travel throughout Europe. In a letter to a friend at Christmastime in 1921, Hemingway bragged:

> Living is very cheap. Hotel room is 12 francs and there are 12.61 to the paper one (dollar bill). A meal for two hits a male about 12–14 francs—about 50 cents apiece. Wine is 60 centimes. Good Pinard. I get rum for 14 francs a bottle. Vive la France.

He was more succinct in the *Toronto Star Weekly* a few weeks later: "Paris in the winter is rainy, cold, beautiful and cheap. It is also noisy, jostling, crowded and cheap. It is anything you want—and cheap." He added, "At the present rate of exchange, a Canadian with an income of one thousand dollars a year can live comfortably and enjoyably in Paris. If exchange were normal the same Canadian would starve to death. Exchange is a wonderful thing."

Canadian expat John Glassco agreed:

> Here I must say that I don't think the rate of exchange is always given its proper importance as an element in the charm of Paris: to be able to live well on very little money is the best basis for an appreciation of beauty anywhere, and I think we admired the city all the more because we could now eat and drink almost as much as we liked.

Thousands of Americans sailed to France each year during the 1920s. Vintage postcard, celebrating the SS France's *1921 maiden voyage.* FROM THE AUTHOR'S COLLECTION.

THE BRONX

¾ ounce London dry gin
¾ ounce dry vermouth
¾ ounce sweet vermouth
½ ounce fresh orange juice (recipe calls for the
juice of a quarter orange)
1 dash orange bitters
Orange peel, for garnish

Shake well with ice, then strain into a chilled cocktail glass. Garnish with an orange peel.

Recipe from Cocktails de Paris *(1929)*.

NEW YORK CITY BOASTS CLASSIC COCKTAILS NAMED for four of its five boroughs. The first, of course, was the Manhattan, and you've also got the Bronx, the Brooklyn, and Queens. To date, I'm not aware of a (good) drink called the Staten Island, but I could be wrong. But this is a book about Paris, not New York. The Bronx was quite popular worldwide, and especially among a few of the members of the Lost Generation.

In his 1920 classic, *This Side of Paradise*, F. Scott Fitzgerald has his protagonist Amory Blaine drinking more than a few of these to ease a heartbreak. He's at New York's Knickerbocker Bar, "his head spinning gorgeously, layer upon layer of soft satisfaction setting over the bruised spots of his spirit."

John Dos Passos recalled dining with F. Scott and Zelda, and later wrote that "there was a golden innocence about them and they were

Cover of the 1929 book Cocktails de Paris. IMAGE COURTESY OF EXPOSITION UNIVERSELLE DES VINS ET SPIRITUEUX.

both so helplessly goodlooking [*sic*]. . . . As I remember we drank Bronx cocktails, and then champagne."

Want to guess what cocktail young Ernest Hemingway and Hadley Richardson enjoyed on one of their first dates in 1920? According to a letter Hemingway sent to his pal Bill Smith, the young couple had dinner at Chicago's Victor House, which included "two Rounds of Bronix's [*sic*]," they then "went to the College Inn and danced. We were in the finest of shape. It was a jovial affair."

In a 1922 *Toronto Daily Star* piece, Hemingway commented favorably on the state of mixology in the City of Light as "the present blissful time when the French bartender has at last learned to mix a good martini and a palate-soothing bronx."

The Bronx peaked during Prohibition, it seems. In 1934, *Esquire* magazine included it in its list of the "Ten Worst Cocktails" of the

1920s, and the *New York Sun*'s G. Selmer Fougner, in his "Along the Wine Trail" column, speculated that because "everyone had gin, everyone had orange juice, and by the 1930s everyone was sick of the combination."

But we'll leave it to poet and publisher Harry Crosby, an unabashed fan of the Bronx, for the final word. His diary entry from February 10, 1924, begins:

> Credo, I believe—that a Bronx cocktail is the best drink, the newspapers are an abomination, that the sea is marvelous from the vantage point of the beach and horses marvelous from the vantage point of the ground, that violets and gardenias are the most perfumed, that woman is the slave to man and also all his "joye and blisse," that life is a black sadness powdered with suns of gold.

Bartender Louis Fouquet created his own Parisian variation on the Bronx, way back in the 1890s, and you'd likely still find it in the 1920s. Fouquet's Louis Cocktail, from his groundbreaking 1896 book *Bariana*, went like this:

LOUIS COCKTAIL

1 ounce London dry gin
1 ounce sweet vermouth
1 ounce fresh orange juice
3 dashes orange curaçao
3 dashes Angostura aromatic bitters
3 dashes crème de noyaux
Lemon peel and maraschino cherry, for garnish

Stir well with ice, then strain into a chilled cocktail glass, garnish with lemon peel and maraschino cherry.

☛ **TASTING NOTE:** The Bronx is a bit of a period piece, reflecting some of the popular flavors of the pre-Prohibition era (the gin-and-orange platform, particularly). Using freshly squeezed orange juice is the key, and you can moderate the sweetness by regulating the sweet vermouth and/or the curaçao. If you're making the Louis Cocktail, Tempus Fugit Spirits or Noyau de Poissy are both solid examples of crème de noyaux.

THE BUÑUELONI

(and other Negroni variations)

---

1 ounce Campari
1 ounce sweet vermouth
¾ ounce London dry gin
Orange wedge or twist, for garnish

Stir all ingredients well in a mixing glass with ice, then strain into a rocks glass filled with fresh ice. Garnish with orange wedge or twist.

THE NEGRONI HAS EMERGED AS ONE OF THE MORE popular drinks on today's cocktail scene. But was it found in 1920s Paris? Yes. Well, sort of. Mindful of Shakespeare's line about how "a rose by any other name would smell as sweet," we do find a few Negroni-esque drinks lurking about the streets of Paris under assumed names.

We'll start with a drink favored by Spanish filmmaker Luis Buñuel. He came to Paris in 1925, and collaborated with Salvador Dalí, a colleague from his university days, in making the groundbreaking short film *Un Chien Andalou* (1929). It was not your conventional film, and featured, among other things, a woman's eye being sliced by a razor blade.

Buñuel and Dalí wrote the script in six days at Dalí's home in Cadaqués, Spain, a coastal village near the French border. Buñuel later recalled how the plot evolved: "Dalí said to me, 'I dreamed last night of ants swarming around my hands,' and I said, 'Good Lord,

1926 Campari ad.
IMAGE COURTESY OF
DAVID CAMPARI-MILANO.

and I dreamed that I sliced somebody or other's eye. There's the film, let's go make it.'" As Buñuel further noted, "Our only rule was very simple: no idea or image that might lend itself to a rational explanation of any kind would be accepted. We had to open all doors to the irrational and keep only those images that surprised us, without trying to explain why."

After the film's premiere, Buñuel and Dalí were warmly embraced by Paris's burgeoning surrealist movement, led by poet André Breton. At the film's original screening, Buñuel played a sequence of phonograph records, alternating between Argentinian tangos and Wagner's *Tristan und Isolde*, that he switched manually while keeping his pockets full of stones with which to pelt would-be hecklers.

It seems fitting that a drink with such bold and dynamic flavors would be embraced by a man who made such provocative films. Buñuel explained that this concoction was intended "to be drunk in a bar in mid-afternoon." He defined the perfect bar as "an exercise in solitude. It must be quiet, dark, and very comfortable—no music of any kind, not more than a dozen tables and a client that doesn't like to talk."

Buñuel never missed his daily cocktail, since "where certain things are concerned I plan ahead." Just as with those rocks in his pockets, it's quite obvious to me that, like a good Boy Scout, Buñuel was always prepared.

Other Parisian drinks that played on the Negroni included the Camparinete, made with 1½ ounces of Gordon's gin, and ¼ ounce each of Campari and Cora Stravei sweet vermouth, and finished with a zest of lemon peel. It's found in the 1929 book *Cocktails de Paris*, by Georges Gabriel Thenon. It's attributed to Albert, a bartender at the Hôtel Chatham's bar.*

Another Negroni variation was the Tunnel Cocktail, invented at Harry's New York Bar, and first seen in *ABC of Mixing Cocktails* (1930). It contains one ounce each of London dry gin and Campari, and then a half ounce each of sweet and dry vermouth, with an orange peel squeezed on top. According to *Barflies*, "This cocktail was awarded Prix d'Honneur at the International Bartenders' Contest, Paris, 1929. *(Recipe by Bob Card, Harry's New York Bar, Paris)*."

And finally, the cocktail book *L'Heure du Cocktail: Recettes pour 1929*, by J. Alimbau and E. Milhorat, offered three Negroni variations: the Campari Cocktail, the Campari Mixte, and the Campari Cardinal, each with different ratios of the sacred trinity of gin, Campari, and sweet vermouth.

☞ **TASTING NOTE:** This drink allows you to play around with the ratios, use a little less gin if you find it too strong, for example. Further, you can work in different apéritif bitters for variety.

---

* See also Rose Cocktail (page 170).

CHAMBÉRY FRAISE / FRAISETTE

2 ounces vermouth (blanc or dry)
1 ounce strawberry liqueur, syrup, or several
slices of ripe strawberry
Seltzer water, to top off
Lemon peel or fresh strawberry, for garnish

Add vermouth and strawberry liqueur to a tall glass filled with ice, top with seltzer water, stir, and serve. Garnish with lemon peel or fresh strawberry.

Recipe from Barflies and Cocktails *(1927).*

C HAMBÉRY IS A CITY IN SOUTHEASTERN FRANCE. BUT in the days before modern-day France and Italy, both Chambéry and nearby Turin, Italy, were cities in the kingdom of Savoy. With the invention of (sweet) vermouth in Turin in 1786,* it naturally spread to Chambéry, where a lighter and drier style was created, with Dolin as its first producer. By the middle of the nineteenth century, the blanc style of Chambéry was embraced in Paris. It became popular to add strawberries, and by the twentieth century, seltzer water and ice were added.

It bears several names, Chambéry fraise / Fraisette, or vermouth

---

* See also Vermouth Cocktail (page 221).

fraise / Fraisette. In older recipes, "Fraisette" implied the inclusion of a now-defunct brand of strawberry liqueur. Additionally, according to Eric Seed, owner of Dolin's importer, Haus Alpenz, "By the 1920s, most Chambéry producers had a strawberry puree–infused vermouth, and these sold well throughout France." Dolin currently offers Chambéryzette, a strawberry-flavored vermouth blanc, though it's not yet exported to the States.

The Chambéry Fraise is mentioned in many of the writings of the day. You find the characters enjoying them in Montmartre in F. Berkeley Smith's 1916 novel, *Babette*, and in Djuna Barnes's 1936 novel, *Nightwood*. Further, when editor and literary critic Gilbert Seldes and his wife, Alice Hall, honeymooned on the Riviera in 1924, they spent an evening with F. Scott and Zelda Fitzgerald enjoying a few glasses of Chambéry Fraise. In his 1970 book, *Memoirs of Montparnasse*, John Glassco recalled an evening in Montparnasse, when "we took a table on the Dôme terrace and drank Chambéry-Fraise."

Humorist S. J. Perelman, who cowrote the screenplays for several Marx Brothers' films, recalled a visit to the Closerie des Lilas, where he "had had three mild infusions of a life-giving fluid called Chambéry Fraise and felt a reasonable degree of self-satisfaction."

> ☛ **TASTING NOTE:** If you can't find a strawberry liqueur or syrup, simply slice up one or two ripe strawberries, muddle them in a shaker, add the vermouth and ice, shake well, then strain over fresh ice cubes, then top with chilled seltzer water. For a true Chambéry-style vermouth, Dolin Blanc and Dolin Dry are recommended.

ROBERT McALMON AND JAMES JOYCE'S BIG NIGHT OUT

Robert McAlmon was not only one of James Joyce's many publishers and benefactors; he was also one of his drinking buddies. Typically, Joyce stuck to white wine; in fact, poet Archibald MacLeish saw to it that every Christmas Sylvia Beach would purchase on his behalf a case of Alsatian wine for Joyce. But one epic night, Joyce and McAlmon made their way "through the list of French drinks," perhaps including the Chambéry Fraise.

McAlmon was somewhat leery of benders with Joyce, out of a sense of literary responsibility. As Joyce neared completion of *Ulysses*, he suffered from eye trouble. Further, he didn't want to incur the wrath of Joyce's long-suffering wife, Nora, who warned McAlmon, "It's you who see him in a jolly state, but it's me who has to bear the brunt of it if his eyes get ailing, and what a martyr that man can be, you've no idea!" So McAlmon promised Nora and the literary world "never to take him out drinking again for fear of further damaging his health and the book. But that decision was useless." Why? Because, as McAlmon reasoned, "Like myself, when Joyce wants to drink he will drink."

Their epic night began at Gypsy's in the Latin Quarter. Here, McAlmon, Joyce, and his friend Frank Budgen were joined by poet Mina Loy and Djuna Barnes. McAlmon recalled, "Joyce and Budgen were a few drinks ahead of me, but I, having the zeal of youth, quickly caught up." First Budgen left, then Loy and Barnes. Not wanting to call it a night, Joyce and McAlmon stayed "until five in the morning, when the *patron** told us to get out." They ended up "in a small bistro on the Boulevard St.-Germain," where someone thought it would be a good idea to buy cigars. McAlmon continued:

---

* "*Patron*" literally means "boss" in French, but in this and other instances herein it means "manager."

As we decided to drink through the list of French drinks, Joyce began dropping cigars. At first I leaned to pick them up and return them to him. When I could no longer lean without falling on my face I took to lighting the cigars and handing them to him. He almost immediately dropped them, and I lighted cigar after cigar until they were all gone, and then we took to cigarettes. At ten in the morning we sat alone in the small bistro, the floor covered with some twenty cigars, innumerable cigarettes, and the table with the forty glasses which had held our various drinks. The *patron* . . . could not believe that such animals as we had ever lived.

They finally started for home. As McAlmon helped the slumping Joyce up the stairs to his apartment, Nora met them at the door. She ruefully looked at her husband and said, "Jim, you've been doin' this for twenty years, and I am tellin' you it's the end. Do you understand? You've been bringin' your drunken companions to me too long, and now you've started McAlmon in the same way." McAlmon limped back to his own hotel, "to sleep, to die, to know agony, to curse Joyce, life, myself." He later wrote, "It took me three months to get my health mildly into order after that night."

As an aside, more than one writer had wild nights with Joyce, and felt the wrath of Nora. Ernest Hemingway recalled, "We would go out to drink and Joyce would fall into a fight. He couldn't even see the man so he'd say: 'Deal with him, Hemingway! Deal with him!'" When Hemingway brought Joyce "home after a protracted drinking bout, his wife, Nora, would open the door and say, 'well, here comes James Joyce the author, drunk again with Ernest Hemingway.'"

So, the bottom line is, these French apéritif cocktails are lower in alcohol, meaning you can have more than one. Just don't have, you know, *forty* of them. And take it easy with those cigars, too.

CHAMPAGNE

The Obligatory Drink of Montmartre

ALTHOUGH THERE WERE CERTAINLY VENUES FOR LIVE music and dancing elsewhere in Paris (such as Le Jockey in Montparnasse and Le Boeuf sur le Toit near the Madeleine church [page 40]), if you really wanted to let your hair down, have a few drinks, and hear some genuine jazz, you had to go "up the hill" to Montmartre. And Champagne was typically what you'd be drinking. As was noted in *Paris with the Lid Lifted*, "At every after-midnight place, you can buy Champagne only." The *Baltimore Sun* confirmed this in a bit of captured conversation. "Dear, do we have to order champagne?" To which her partner replied, "Now, we can't do Montmartre on the cheap. You've got to order champagne at all these joints—they don't serve anything else." Another guide quipped, "A bottle of champagne must be on every table."

As young *Toronto Daily Star* correspondent Ernest Hemingway noted, "Champagne is the great symbol of nightlife to the uninitiated. And the tourist traps make the most of it. They sell champagne and champagne only. If the visitor tries to order anything else, he is given the choice of champagne or the street door." Indeed, Hemingway would conclude that "champagne is the *deus ex machina* of the after-hours existence of Paris." He further wrote: "After the cork has popped on the third bottle and the jazz band has brayed the

American . . . into such a state of exaltation that he begins to sway slightly with the glory of it all, he is liable to remark thickly and profoundly: 'So this is Paris!'"

You might have gone to a joint called Florence's, on rue Blanche. *Paris with the Lid Lifted* called it "the real, ripping, hotsy-totsy place of Paris, this one," and promised that "you will have one of your best nights in Paris, at Florence's." The entire band and staff were black. "Frisco" and the owner, Florence, were the singers. "Frisco has no equal on earth as a shouter, a stepper and a master of ceremonies. Princes, Lords and Dukes come here and love it. Frisco pulls them right out of their chairs, no matter how blazing their coat of arms; and he drags them out into the middle of the floor and they Charleston and Blackbottom and do everything he tells them to do; and in return they plaster 100 franc notes all over his perspiring face."

Or, you might find yourself at l'Acacia, a fabulous nightclub opened by legendary American socialite Elsa Maxwell (who likely invented the scavenger hunt as a party amusement in Paris in 1927) and Edward Molyneux in 1921. Sadly, l'Acacia lasted but a year, with Maxwell admitting that "the trouble was that Molyneux and I were too busy having a good time to check incoming revenue against outgoing expenses." Yeah, that.

Royalty loved Montmartre. You might run into the Duke and Duchess of Windsor at Bricktop's, or the Prince of Wales at Kiley's. Indeed, the Prince "likes to show that one can be heir to the throne of England and yet be none the less of a gay boulevardier for all that. Every time he has a little time to spare he comes across the Channel and spends several days in Paris, never going to bed before six in the morning. On these happy evenings he may be seen merrily dancing all over Montmartre."

As you might expect, an evening in Montmartre might end up a blur, as eloquently expressed by the immortal Basil Woon: "By this time you have caught the Paris fever—the itch is in your foot. So just one more bottle—how many have we had?"

F. Scott Fitzgerald ruefully recalled many lost nights in Montmartre in his short story "Babylon Revisited," which concerns a man

1893 G. H. Mumm & Co. Champagne advertisement from 1893, used extensively in 1920s Paris. IMAGE COURTESY OF PERNOD-RICARD.

who is reassessing his Paris days. He's older and wiser, and more than a little nostalgic. After a visit to the Casino to watch "Josephine Baker go through her chocolate arabesques," he headed for Montmartre. "He passed a lighted door from which issued music, and stopped with the sense of familiarity; it was Bricktop's, where he had parted with so many hours and so much money." He walked farther down the street, warily entering a cabaret. "Immediately an eager orchestra burst into sound, a pair of professional dancers leaped to their feet and a maître d'hôtel swooped toward him, crying, 'Crowd just arriving, sir!'" But he withdrew quickly. "'You have to be damn drunk,' he thought."

But it wasn't just up in Montmartre that the bubbly was flowing. Indeed, at its grand opening, some twenty-five hundred revelers came to La Coupole on boulevard Montparnasse the evening of

Vintage postcard from La Coupole, boulevard Montparnasse. FROM THE AUTHOR'S COLLECTION.

December 20, 1927, where some twelve hundred bottles of Mumm Champagne were consumed.

Other denizens of Paris were Champagne enthusiasts as well. Novelist Marcel Proust was quoted as saying, "While drinking a bottle of Veuve Clicquot Champagne, I could feel happiness penetrating my whole existence." Famed dancer Isadora Duncan gave artist Tsuguharu Foujita dance lessons in return for Champagne. Hemingway added, "If I have any money, I can't think of any better way of spending money than on champagne." But he was no fan of the smaller, 375-milliliter-size bottle (known as a "split"): "The half bottle of champagne is the enemy of man."

Among my favorite Champagne passages from the pages of 1920s literature would include one from F. Scott Fitzgerald's *The Great Gatsby*, when Nick Carraway confesses, "I was enjoying myself now. I had taken two finger-bowls of champagne, and the scene had changed before my eyes into something significant, elemental, and profound."

And the other? In *The Sun Also Rises*, while Brett, Jake, and Count Mippipopolous are drinking Mumm Champagne, "Brett held up her glass. 'We ought to toast something. Here's to royalty,'" she said. But the Count wisely corrected her. "This wine is too good for toast-drinking, my dear. You don't want to mix emotions up with a wine like that. You lose the taste."

And finally, in gratitude for F. Scott Fitzgerald's assistance in editing the original manuscript of *The Sun Also Rises*, Hemingway was obliged to thank him: "Now I don't owe you anything besides undying gratitude and say 180 bottles of champagne . . ."

☞ **TASTING NOTE:** In France, only sparkling wines from the Champagne region of France may be called by that name. Other sparkling wines are known by the names *mousseux* or *Crémant*. Of course, there's a great variety of sparkling wines from around the world, notably *cavas* from Spain, which offer superb value.

SIX CHARACTERS IN SEARCH OF AN AUTHOR—WITH A GUN!

The year 1926 brought the publication of Hemingway's novel *The Sun Also Rises*. Five years earlier, *Six Characters in Search of an Author* debuted on Broadway (I'll get back to that in a moment). In Hemingway's novel, most of the characters were based on real-life people*; for example, Brett Ashley was based on Duff Twysden, Robert Cohn on Harold Loeb, Mike Campbell on Pat Guthrie, Harvey Stone on Harold Stearns, and Braddocks on Ford Madox Ford, to name a few. To say that most of the characters made the real people look bad would be an understatement. Hemingway even bragged to Kitty Cannell that he was "writing a book with a plot and everything. Everybody's in it. . . . 'But not you, Kitty,' Hemingway promised, 'I'm not going to put you in. I've always said you were a wonderful girl!'" Actually, he *did* put Kitty in it; she was the annoying Frances Clyne.

So the winter of 1926–1927 found Hemingway quite popular on the world's literary stage but a bit of a pariah in Montparnasse. In his memoir, Jimmie Charters deftly referred to the situation as "Six Characters in Search of an Author—with a Gun!" The character who fared the worst had to be Loeb, who allegedly put the word out that he'd kill Hemingway next time he saw him. Hemingway later said that he "sent him a telegram to the effect that I would be here in the Hole in the Wall for three consecutive evenings so he'd have no trouble finding me." This bar was on boulevard des Capucines, and also went by the French name Trou Dans le Mur. Three nights passed and Loeb never showed up. About a week later, Hemingway was dining at Brasserie Lipp when Loeb walked in. Out of reflex, Loeb went to shake Hemingway's hand "before he remembered we

* For an in-depth look at the people behind the characters, see Lesley M. M. Blume's *Everybody Behaves Badly: The True Story Behind Hemingway's Masterpiece* The Sun Also Rises (Boston: Eamon Dolan/Houghton Mifflin Harcourt, 2016).

Trou Dans le Mur,
the "Hole in the Wall" Bar,
23 boulevard des Capucines
(now occupied by Opéra Mandarin).
PHOTOGRAPH BY PAUL ALMASY,
COURTESY OF AKG IMAGES.

were mortal enemies," then pulled his hand away. Nevertheless, Hemingway offered to have a drink with him. Loeb refused. Hemingway shrugged and said, "Okay, then drink alone." Loeb walked away, "and that was the end of the vendetta."

If you read enough Hemingway lore, there are often multiple versions of the same story: his version versus that of the other party. Oddly enough, this story has two versions, Hemingway's and Hemingway's. Indeed, he wrote to F. Scott Fitzgerald that "Loeb was in town and was going to shoot me so I sent word around that I would be found unarmed sitting in front of Lipp's brasserie . . . and everybody who wished to shoot me was to come and do it then or for Christ sake to stop talking about it. No bullets whistled. There was a story around that I had gone to switserland ⟨*sic*⟩ to avoid being shot by demented characters out of my books."

Regardless of the venue, it's a pretty good story. For what it's worth, Hemingway later described the Hole in the Wall as "a hangout for deserters and for dope peddlers during and after the first war . . ." and that it "was a narrow bar, almost a passageway . . . which had, at one time, a rear exit into the sewers of Paris from which you were supposed to be able to reach the catacombs."

CHAMPAGNE COCKTAIL

1 sugar cube
2–3 drops Angostura aromatic bitters
Lemon peel, for garnish
4–5 ounces chilled Champagne or sparkling wine

Place a sugar cube at the bottom of a Champagne flute. Add a few drops of Angostura bitters to saturate the cube. Add one ice cube and a slice of lemon peel. Slowly fill flute with Champagne. Stir and serve.

Recipe from The Artistry of Mixing Drinks *(1936)*.

THE CHAMPAGNE COCKTAIL IS ONE OF THE ALL-TIME classics. It appears in the world's first cocktail book, Jerry Thomas's *How to Mix Drinks* (1862). It's a simple drink to make but rewards your effort with complex flavors and quite a visual show with the dissolving sugar cube throwing off billowing clouds and bubbles.

It's a Paris staple, then and now. The indispensable guide *How to Wine and Dine in Paris* (1930) offered: "What might be called the two Parisian specialties in cocktails are the Rose (page 170) and the Champagne Cocktail. One cannot get a good Champagne Cocktail everywhere, but when it is good it is all that a bibulous taste can desire."

Of all the gin joints in all the towns in the world, the Champagne Cocktail appears most often connected to the Hotel Ritz Paris. In his facetious (though probably true) work *A Short Autobiography*, F. Scott Fitzgerald offered a year-by-year accounting of the more memorable drink-related events of his life (of course, such events weren't always so easy to remember). In 1925, during which he and Zelda moved to Paris, published *The Great Gatsby*, and met Ernest Hemingway, he tersely recorded, "Champagne cocktails in the Ritz sweatshop. . . . Kirsch in a Burgundy inn against the rain* with E. Hemingway."

The memoirs of both Morley Callaghan and Harry Crosby tell of evenings at the Ritz with Champagne Cocktails. Callaghan had a few one evening with F. Scott Fitzgerald ("Drinking champagne cocktails, we talked on until after six . . ."), while Crosby's was a bit more decadent:

> We drank champagne cocktails (three each) and then we went to the Ritz for some more (two each) then to Le Doyen's [*sic*] (three each) then to the Ballet Russe (very poor) then to the Jungle for gin and dancing (great fun) and they played marvelous jazz and it was hot and alive (Irene hot and alive) . . . and I love this madness.

Novelist John Dos Passos had his characters drinking Champagne Cocktails at the Ritz in his 1932 novel, *Nineteen Nineteen*, as did Anita Loos, in her 1925 book, *Gentlemen Prefer Blondes*:

> So we came to the Ritz Hotel and the Ritz Hotel was divine. Because when a girl can sit in a delightful bar and have delicious champagne cocktails and look at all the important French people in Paris, I think it is divine.

Zelda Fitzgerald agreed; she loved Champagne Cocktails, which "were for her the mark of urban sophistication." Maurice Chevalier was known to enjoy them at Paris's famous restaurant Maxim's. And composer Cole Porter was also such a fan that Michael Arlen, author of the bestselling 1924 novel *The Green Hat*, offered the following caricature:

> Every morning at half-past seven Cole Porter leaps lightly out of bed and, having said his prayers, arranges himself in a riding habit. Then, having written a song or two, he will appear at the stroke of half-past twelve at the Ritz, where leaning in a manly way on the bar,

---

* See also Whiskey Sour (page 233).

Elegant dining in the Ritz's Le Petit Jardin, "the little garden." In later years, Hemingway wrote that "when I dream of an afterlife in Paris, the action always takes place in the Paris Ritz. It's a fine summer night. I knock back a couple of martinis in the bar Rue Cambon side. Then there's a wonderful dinner under a flowering chestnut tree in what's called Le Petit Jardin. That's the little garden that faces the Grill." VINTAGE POSTCARD FROM THE AUTHOR'S COLLECTION.

he will say, "Champagne cocktail, please. Had a marvelous ride this morning!" That statement gives him strength and confidence on which to suffer this, our life, until ten minutes past three in the afternoon when he will fall into a childlike sleep.

☛ **TASTING NOTE:** You can have a lot of fun with this classic by varying the types of bitters you use. Have a few friends over, each bringing a bottle of sparkling wine. Put out a bowl of sugar cubes, along with all the bitters you have, and try the drink with Angostura, maybe Regans' orange bitters, Peychaud's bitters, or Fee Brothers Whiskey Barrel-Aged bitters, or others. They'll each add a new dynamic to a venerable old drink.

COLE PORTER AND
ADA "BRICKTOP" SMITH

Cole Porter, one of the greatest twentieth-century songwriters, lived much of his life in Paris, and his 1929 musical, *Fifty Million Frenchmen*, served as homage to his adopted home. A close friend of Gerald and Sara Murphy (he and Gerald were Yale alums), Sara described Cole as "a natural-born hedonist . . . he wanted to live like a king which was all right too." And that he did. Cole and his wife, Linda, lived a life of opulence and split their time in Paris, Venice, and the Riviera. Their Left Bank home "had platinum wallpaper and chairs upholstered in zebra skin. Mr. Porter once hired the entire Monte Carlo Ballet to entertain his house guests."

And, of course, Porter didn't always have to have Champagne Cocktails. Just plain old Champagne would suffice. Fellow bon vivant Lucius Beebe summed it up pretty well: "It is really the simple things in life which give pleasure to Mr. Porter—half-million-dollar strings of pearls. Isotta motor cars, double bottles of Grand Chambertin '87 . . ."

In addition to being an ardent patron of the Ritz, Porter loved to head "up the hill" to Montmartre to Ada "Bricktop" Smith's joint for live jazz. When he learned that she knew how to dance the Charleston, which was all the rage, he exclaimed, "I'm going to give Charleston cocktail parties at my house two or three times a week, and you're going to teach everyone to dance the Charleston!" Her students included the Porters, socialite Elsa Maxwell, the Aga Khan, members of the Vanderbilt and Rothschild families, as well as the Duchess of Marlborough. Their friendship endured, and he later composed a song for Bricktop to sing, "Miss Otis Regrets."

DÔME COCKTAIL

¾ ounce Dubonnet
¾ ounce London dry gin
⅜ ounce anisette
1 teaspoon orgeat*

Stir well with ice, then strain into a chilled cocktail glass.

Recipe from ABC of Mixing Cocktails *(1934).*

THIS DRINK WAS CREATED BY RAY CAREY, "WHO POURED drinks for Americans throughout the twenties and thirties." A former ranch hand near the California-Mexico border, he joined the U.S. Army and came to France during World War I. Like so many, he remained in Paris, and soon became head bartender at the Café du Dôme. In 1936, Ray opened his own place, the Bar Basque, at 10 rue Delambre, the former address of the former Dingo.

The Café du Dôme opened in 1898 and soon became a renowned gathering place for intellectuals, artists, and bohemians, attracting the likes of painter Paul Gauguin, philosopher Khalil Gibran, Max Ernst, and most if not all the other notables mentioned elsewhere in this book.

As more and more Anglo-Americans came to Paris after World War I, the hospitality industry of Montparnasse took steps to accommodate them. In late 1921, the Rotonde was renovated and greatly

---

* Orgeat syrup is used as a sweetener in cocktails, similar to simple syrup but also including (natural or artificial) almond flavoring.

expanded. In February 1924, Ernest and Hadley Hemingway attended "the opening of the newly designed and renovated" Café du Dôme, "now glitzy and more expensive, trying to attract American tourists rather than locals, writers and artists." The Paris edition of the *Chicago Tribune* snarkily described it as "now as up-to-date, modern, shiny and completely equipped as the bath room in the home of an American 'Babbitt,'" a veiled reference to Sinclair Lewis, who decidedly was not a fan of the Dôme.

Down the street, at 10 rue Delambre, the Dingo got its "Americanization" in 1923, Le Sélect opened in 1925, and the café La Coupole opened to great fanfare in December 1927. These classic watering holes, along with the nearby Falstaff and Jockey, made the intersection of rue Delambre and the boulevards Montparnasse and Raspail (known as the Carrefour Vavin) the social epicenter of the Anglo-American arts community of the era. While the Dingo and Jockey are sadly no more, the Dôme, Rotonde, La Coupole, Le Falstaff, and Le Sélect remain today, allowing one to sit on the terrace and imagine the scene as it might have been ninety or so years ago.

Now known as Restaurant Le Dôme, it's come a long way from its humble origins as "merely a zinc bar with a small terrace." It's now a world-class, Michelin-rated seafood restaurant, with a top-flight wine and beverage program.

☞ **TASTING NOTE:** This is sort of a fancied-up version of the classic Dubonnet cocktail, said to be the "pre-lunch cocktail of choice" of Queen Elizabeth II. The orgeat syrup is optional, as there's enough sweetness in the Dubonnet to balance out the drink. Up to you, of course. You might also try Byrrh in place of Dubonnet, as it is more reflective of a quinquina from 1920s Paris.

As a final comment on the drink, go judiciously on the anisette, as it can overpower the flavor.

FRENCH 75

WHILE TODAY WE CALL THIS THE FRENCH 75, IN 1920S Paris it was simply the 75, or the *soixante-quinze*, which is French for, you guessed it, "seventy-five." See, they'd never call it the French 75 in Paris, just as Parisians would never call their beloved *pommes frites* something as vulgar as french fries. And in addition to being called by several names, there are several distinctly different recipes, on both sides of the Atlantic.* The recipe shown above is how they made it at the Ritz Bar, but at Harry's New York Bar, it was quite different.

---

* Go see Chris Hannah at New Orleans's French 75 Bar; he'll make you one with Cognac, not gin.

THE 75 COCKTAIL—HARRY'S NEW YORK BAR VERSION

1½ ounces Calvados or apple brandy
¾ ounce London dry gin
1 teaspoon grenadine
2 dashes absinthe

Shake well, then strain into a chilled cocktail glass.

Recipe from Barflies and Cocktails *(1927)*.

The Harry's version was very close to the first one to appear in print, both in newspapers and in cocktail books. The December 4, 1915, edition of the *Wilmington Morning News* reported that:

> There has been brought back to Broadway from the front by war correspondent E. Alexander Powell the Soixante-Quinze cocktail—the French Seventy-five. It is one-third gin, one-third grenadine, one-third applejack, and a dash of lemon juice. Frank Leon Smith, the story writer, says he drank one and immediately paid the rent.

And you'll find a similar gin-and-Calvados recipe in Robert Vermeire's 1922 classic, *Cocktails: How to Mix Them*, and in Adolphe Torelli's 1927 book, *900 Recettes de Cocktails et Boissons Americaines*. Vermeire stated that the drink "was introduced by Henry of Henry's bar fame in Paris."* For the sake of argument, the *Galveston Daily News* of May 17, 1923, attributed the drink to Frank Meier at the Ritz, though Meier doesn't claim ownership in *The Artistry of Mixing Drinks*, published in 1936.

What we can agree on is that the drink derives its name from the French army's 75 mm artillery gun, used extensively in both

---

* For more about Henry's, see Vermouth and Seltzer (page 210).

French soldiers struggle to reposition the Soixante-Quinze,
the legendary 75 mm artillery piece, in battle.
VINTAGE POSTCARD FROM THE AUTHOR'S COLLECTION.

world wars. Humorist Irvin S. Cobb, a war correspondent for the *Saturday Evening Post*, offered this bon mot: "I had my first of these in a dugout in the Argonne. I couldn't tell whether a shell or the drink hit me." Every bit as witty, in his 1930 classic, *The Savoy Cocktail Book*, Harry Craddock noted that the drink "hits with remarkable precision."

In case you're wondering, "So the French 75 made with gin, Champagne, sugar, and lemon juice? Isn't that from Paris?" I'll defer to cocktail guru David Wondrich on that one: "The French 75 as we know it first appears in print in 1927, at the height of Prohibition, in a bootlegger-friendly little volume called *Here's How*, put out by a New York humor magazine. From there, it got picked up by the 1930 *Savoy Cocktail Book*, and once it was in there, it was everywhere."

THE 1930 RECIPE FROM
THE SAVOY COCKTAIL BOOK

1½ ounces London dry gin
¾ ounce fresh lemon juice
1 teaspoon sugar
Champagne, to top off

Pour into tall glass containing cracked ice and fill up with Champagne.

☛ **TASTING NOTE:** The Ritz recipe is more like the French 75 that you'll find today, with the Pernod acting as a flavor enhancer. The Harry's version is an interesting drink; the gin and apple brandy work well together. Use Laird's Straight Applejack 86 or their Rare Apple Brandy, or a good Calvados for more flavor, and be careful with the absinthe, as it can dominate. A different style of gin, such as Hayman's Old Tom, adds a new dimension.

GIN FIZZ

2 ounces London dry gin
½ ounce fresh lemon juice
1 teaspoon sugar
2–4 ounces soda water
Mint, for garnish "in the Riviera manner" (optional)

Shake well with ice, then strain into a Delmonico (short) glass, top with chilled soda water.

Recipe from The Artistry of Mixing Drinks *(1936).*

THE GIN FIZZ WAS A STAPLE IN 1920s PARIS, AND YOU can still get a pretty good one there today. The savvy bartenders of Paris saw fit to offer American expats this delicious drink. And it wasn't just the barmen; indeed, the *Brooklyn Daily Eagle* reported the following in 1926:

> That thirsty ladies shall not have to suffer drought while having their hair bobbed, an enterprising Paris hair dresser has installed a bar in his shop. While madame is taking a "permanent" or a bob curl, she may sip a cocktail or a gin fizz in perfect comfort. And she will be in a more hospitable frame of mind when . . . she receives the bill.

The Gin Fizz was a favorite of writer / publisher / man-about-town Robert McAlmon, who drank them on the terrace at the Dôme (on one occasion, joined by "two girls who looked like walking wax models"), at the Swedish restaurant the Stryx (with Sinclair Lewis's

Brasserie Lipp, on the boulevard Saint-Germain, Left Bank. Where John Glassco said they "served the best gin fizz in town," and Ernest Hemingway went to enjoy a decadent, well-deserved lunch after receiving one of his first paychecks for a work of nonfiction. VINTAGE POSTCARD FROM THE AUTHOR'S COLLECTION.

wife Gracie), and with writer Kay Boyle at Le Grand Ecart. McAlmon's friend John Glassco "remembered hearing that the Brasserie Lipp served the best gin fizz in town and I went inside and ordered one."

Harry Crosby also fancied an occasional Gin Fizz (it might be easier to find a cocktail he *didn't* drink). His memoirs find him enjoying them at the Ritz, and also having a few Gin Fizzes and Sherry Cobblers (page 183) while waiting for his friend and fellow poet Hart Crane to be released from La Santé Prison. The following diary entry truly captures Harry's personality:

We drank gin fizzes and took cold baths and put rouge on our toenails.

Or this one:

A miraculous luncheon gin fizzes and *oeufs suzette* and coffee ice cream and still the effects of the opium pill . . .

A short story Dorothy Parker wrote for the *New Yorker* in 1929 features a pair of crass American tourists on holiday in the South of France: "The two young New Yorkers sat on the cool terrace that rose sharp from the Mediterranean, and looked into deep gin fizzes, embellished, in the Riviera manner, with mint." It seems they were doing their best to dress in the local style, unfortunately a mishmash of different regions of France: "They wore bérets, striped fishing-shirts, wide-legged cotton trousers, and rope-soled espadrilles." Parker compared it to "a Frenchman, summering at an American resort" and wearing "a felt sombrero, planter's overalls, and rubber hip-boots."

While I'm sure it was accidental, F. Scott and Zelda Fitzgerald allowed their three-year-old daughter, Scottie, to drink a Gin Fizz. In the words of her father: "We bathed the daughter in the *bidet* by mistake and she drank the gin fizz thinking it was lemonade . . ." But Zelda did say, after all, that she wanted to raise Scottie as a flapper, "because flappers are brave and gay and beautiful."

The head bartender of the Ritz, Frank Meier, offered his own variation on this classic. He called it Frank's Special Gin Fizz, and he added "one quarter of crushed peach."

☞ **TASTING NOTE:** As with any other drink in this book, be sure to use freshly squeezed juice. You might also take a page from Frank Meier's book, adding fruit to the mix, such as some ripe blackberries or strawberries—shake the gin, lemon, and ice before adding the sparkling water.

ROBERT McALMON

Perhaps no American in Paris exemplified the expat experience more than writer and publisher Robert McAlmon. He was the quintessential gadabout, the night owl of all night owls. As early as 1924, he was described in the *Asbury Park Press* as "the Play-Boy of the literary world. One can be fairly sure of finding him within 100 yards of the Dôme Café, altho ⟨*sic*⟩ since that caravansary began to redecorate he is most likely to be at the Dingo Bar, around the corner."

But there was so much more to him than legendary drinker. He founded Contact Editions, which published works of Ernest Hemingway, Gertrude Stein, Djuna Barnes, James Joyce, Ezra Pound, and Ford Madox Ford. He also wrote the critically acclaimed collection *A Hasty Bunch.* Sylvia Beach fondly recalled him as "certainly the most popular member of 'the Crowd,' as he called it," referring to Joyce, Hemingway, Nancy Cunard, Jean Cocteau, Nina Hamnett, Ezra Pound, Kay Boyle, Flossie Martin, Jimmie Charters, Harold Loeb, Man Ray, Djuna Barnes, and many others. "Somehow," Beach recalled, "he dominated whatever group he was in. Whatever café or bar McAlmon patronized at the moment was the one where you saw everybody."

He was a benefactor to many in the literary colony. In fact, McAlmon helped Sylvia Beach to gather subscribers for James Joyce's *Ulysses.* She described how he would "comb the night clubs" for prospective purchasers, persuading them to put their signatures— many of them "slightly zigzag" on the order forms. When the book was published many people were surprised to find out they had signed up." Beach also described another form of McAlmon's (shall we say) "patronage," i.e., covering his friends' bar tabs. "The drinks were always on him, and alas! often in him."

For example, guess who paid for the bulk of Hemingway's first-ever visit to see the bullfights of Spain? McAlmon. It was the spring of 1923, and they both took the train from Paris to Madrid, "well lubricated with whisky." After the trip, Hemingway summed up his traveling companion fairly succinctly: "amusements and occupation drinking, nightlife and gossip."

Ernest Hemingway and Robert McAlmon attending the bullfights in Spain, May–June 1923.
PHOTOGRAPH COURTESY OF THE ERNEST HEMINGWAY COLLECTION, JOHN F. KENNEDY PRESIDENTIAL LIBRARY AND MUSEUM, BOSTON.

McAlmon's money came from a somewhat offbeat source. Although a bisexual, he was married to the poet Bryher, née Annie Winifred Ellerman, the daughter of a British shipping magnate. Her parents insisted that she be married, not wanting her to travel Europe alone. They were likely unaware that the couple's marriage wasn't exactly conventional. Heavens no. She lived with her lover, poet Hilda Doolittle (H.D.); they spent most of their time in Switzerland. When their marriage of convenience ended in 1927, McAlmon received a nice financial settlement from Bryher's father, along with a nickname, "Robber McAlimony," perhaps coined by Joyce.

When living in Paris, McAlmon would not fail to miss Bastille Day; "the idea of Paris in drunken festival, and me not one of the drunkest there, was austere." John Glassco recalls an evening out with Bob: "McAlmon's own capacity for alcohol was astounding: within the next half hour he drank half a dozen double whiskies with no apparent effect." Glassco also recounted a classic McAlmon quote, perhaps epitomizing Gertrude Stein's famous remark: "My generation doesn't eat supper. I'm having another drink. Waiter, five whiskies and water!"

Unfortunately, he burned a few bridges along the way. Perhaps it was because he didn't suffer fools, or anything, for that matter. Glassco marveled at McAlmon's rudeness and "total absence of attitude or artifice. . . . He admired no writing of any kind, either ancient or modern; all government was a farce; all people were fools or snobs. He spoke of his friends with utter contempt . . . but all with such an absence of conviction that one could not take him seriously." This perhaps led to the end of a few friendships. When McAlmon spread rumors that both Hemingway and F. Scott Fitzgerald were "fairies," Fitzgerald called him "a bitter rat" and "a pretty good person to avoid." Hemingway said he was "a son of a bitch with a mind like an ingrowing toenail." Aware of McAlmon's binges, and recalling that he was among his early publishers, Hemingway complained to Alice B. Toklas, "I do not like to see him throw up my royalties."

Sadly, McAlmon, once the most popular of the expat colony, died in relative obscurity in Desert Hot Springs, California, in 1956, at the age of sixty.

GIN RICKEY

2 ounces London dry gin
½ ounce fresh lime juice
2–3 ounces seltzer water

Add ingredients to a rocks glass or tumbler, stir and serve. Optional, drop the squeezed lime hull into the glass.

Recipe from Barflies and Cocktails *(1927)*.

THIS IS ANOTHER F. SCOTT AND ZELDA FITZGERALD favorite. Folklore tells us that F. Scott favored gin because he believed it left no odor on his breath, and he featured the Gin Rickey in his 1925 classic, *The Great Gatsby*. In the story, Gatsby and Nick Carraway visit the home of Daisy and Tom Buchanan. Tom is unaware that Gatsby and Daisy had once been lovers, and perhaps still are. It was a "broiling" day, "certainly the warmest, of the summer." Daisy dispatched Tom to "make us some drinks," so that she and Gatsby might have a moment alone. When Tom returned, he brought with him "four gin rickeys that clicked full of ice."

Gatsby took up his drink.
"They certainly look cool," he said, with visible tension.
We drank in long, greedy swallows.

Zelda invented a Rickey-esque drink of her own, composed of "three parts gin, one part water and the juice of a lemon," more or less the same drink, with lemon in place of the lime. And, while discussing the challenge of balancing his craft with the demands of book promotion, F. Scott ruefully noted that "writing and publicity make a lousy gin rickey."

The Gin Rickey had long been a staple in Paris; you'll find it in *Guide du Barman et du Gourmet Chic* (1921) and *American Bar: Recettes des Boissons Anglaises & Américaines* (1900). The original Rickey hails from my Washington, DC, and was invented by (would you believe it?) a Capitol Hill lobbyist, Colonel Joe Rickey, circa 1890. Rickey and other DC politicos used to hang out at a dive bar called Shoomaker's, on Pennsylvania Avenue, just around the corner from the White House. Rickey's Rickey was made with Belle of Nelson Bourbon, lime juice, and Apollinaris mineral water. Over time, it became popular to use gin in place of the Bourbon, and the Gin Rickey is the more common version found today.

☛ **TASTING NOTE:** A pretty straightforward summer-time classic, you might try using naturally flavored sparkling waters to add a little variety, or mineral water, in the manner of the original, 1890s Rickey.

CROG AMERICAIN, A.K.A. HOT RUM PUNCH

1 ounce Cognac
2 ounces dark rum
4 dashes orange curaçao
2 teaspoons sugar
2 dashes fresh lemon juice
Orange, for garnish

Preheat a punch glass. Add the ingredients, then fill the remainder of the punch glass with boiling water and garnish with an orange wheel. Careful, it's hot!

Recipe from American Bar: Recettes des Boissons Anglaises & Américaines *(1900).*

COCKTAIL HISTORIANS CONSIDER PUNCH TO BE THE ancestor of the modern-day cocktail. It dates back hundreds of years, to India, and the name itself derives from the Hindustani word "*panch*," which means "five." So, a properly made punch should have five ingredients: spirit, citrus, tea, sugar, and water.

Of course, it can't always be April in Paris. Winter happens. Then and now, café owners want to keep their terraces open, "for the weather has got to be very bad indeed to drive the Parisian inside a café." In the 1920s, a café had three ways to warm its customers: blankets, charcoal-burning heaters called *braziers*,* and Grog *Americain*, the local name for hot rum punch.

In the classic 1930 guidebook *How to Wine and Dine in Paris*, Robert Forrest Wilson noted that, "the grogs and rums . . . winter apéritifs these, drunk steaming hot with sugar, and a slice of lemon, and only mildly intoxicating, because the heating drives off the alcohol. The French set great store by hot grog as a preventive of influenza. The most celebrated is 'Grog Américain . . .'"

You'll find a few "hot rum grog" references in Harry Crosby's memoirs. Apparently it was a staple for him at the horse races. On October 6, 1928, he noted: "Much sniffing and taking of aspirin tablets and to Longchamp with Esmé (she also sniffling) and we drank hot rum grogs and it was grey and dark . . . and we drank hot rum grogs at the Cascades," referring to a restaurant within the nearby Bois du Boulogne. And perhaps no finer stream of consciousness cocktail story exists in all the land than Harry's July 4, 1927, entry:

> Strong Sun and hot even at sunset and supper in our bathing suits on the beach and the warm sand and cocktails and the cool sand and champagne and the cold sand and midnight a hundred yards off shore and the bewildering lights from the Casino dancing dancing on the water . . . as we swam back to the beach and to Biarritz and the Bar Basque and the strongest hot grog (cold from the swim and tired by the sun and dizzy from the rum).

Cole Porter was also a fan; you'll find a cheeky reference to punch in his 1919 song "My Houseboat on the Thames," which includes the lines, "We'll have punch on board, I think / One to read, and one to drink," referring also to the popular magazine *Punch*.

The drink was commonly found in literature of the day, where it was served at La Closerie des Lilas and at Café des Deux Magots. And as a young journalist with the *Toronto Daily Star*, Ernest Hemingway offered a nice description of a Paris winter's day:

---

* See page 44 for a vintage Byrrh ad showing a charcoal brazier.

Paris with the snow falling. Paris with the big charcoal braziers outside the cafés, glowing red. At the café tables, men huddled, their coat collars turned up, while they finger glasses of grog *Americain* and the newsboys shout the evening papers.

Hemingway offered a similar portrait to publisher Harriet Monroe in a November 16, 1922, letter, where he noted that "the hot rum punch and checker season has come in. It looks like a good winter. Cafes much fuller in the day time now with people that have no heat in their hotel rooms." Indeed, it might have been the first drink he and Hadley enjoyed upon moving to Paris in December of 1921, as you'll see from a letter he wrote to Sherwood Anderson:

> Well here we are. And we sit outside the Dome Cafe, opposite the Rotunde [*sic*] that's being redecorated, warmed up against one of those char-coal brazziers [*sic*] and it's so damned cold outside and the brazier makes it so warm and we drink rum punch, hot, and the rhum enters into us like the Holy Spirit.

Café du Dôme, where Hemingway likely had his first-ever drink in Paris. Located at the heart of the so-called Carrefour Vavin, where boulevards Montparnasse and Raspail intersect with rue Delambre, the epicenter of expat life in the 1920s. VINTAGE POSTCARD FROM THE AUTHOR'S COLLECTION.

Hemingway also worked the drink into his 1926 novel, *The Sun Also Rises*. Jake Barnes and Bill Gorton were in the Spanish village of Burguete en route to Pamplona. It was a cold, blustery evening, and their inn was not well heated. Bill played the piano to keep warm and suggested to Jake, "How about a hot rum punch? . . . This isn't going to keep me warm permanently." So Jake "went out and told the woman what a rum punch was and how to make it." They "drank the hot punch and listened to the wind." When Bill noted that "there isn't too much rum" in the punch, Jake took matters into his own hands and helped himself to the bottle, adding half a glass more to the punch. "Direct action," said Bill. "It beats legislation."

☛ **TASTING NOTE:** Similar to the Bloody Mary, this classic can be varied depending on what you have on hand. All you really need are rum, citrus, and a little sugar, but the addition of Cognac really gives this drink sophistication and structure. Papa's Pilar Dark or Plantation Original Dark are both solid choices in this one, as is Pierre Ferrand Ambre Cognac.

HARRY CROSBY'S BAL DES QUAT'Z'ARTS "TREMENDOUS PUNCH"

---

2 bottles chilled Champagne or sparkling wine
(2¹/₂ ounces to make one drink)
6 ounces London dry gin (¹/₃ ounce)
6 ounces rye whiskey (¹/₃ ounce)
6 ounces Cointreau (¹/₃ ounce)

In a punchbowl add a giant lump of ice, then add the ingredients and place in the refrigerator until cold. Serve in cups. This yields about 18 servings. To make one drink, use the portions in parentheses, stir well with ice, then strain into a cocktail glass.

BEGINNING IN 1892, THE BAL DES QUAT'Z'ARTS, OR THE "Four Arts Ball," has been an institution among the students and patrons of the arts of Paris. In the words of bartender Jimmie Charters, "On the Right Bank the culmination of the spring season was the Grand Prix at the Longchamps racecourse, but on the Left Bank it was the Quat'Z'Arts Ball." Think Mardi Gras meets spring break meets New Year's Eve for the Paris arts community. Charters participated in the 1924 festivities, and his memoirs tell of an uproarious night of drinking and hell-raising.

Joining a group of some 150 revelers, they "marched up the broad boulevard" and "stopped every car that came along, removed from it any girl who seemed attractive, kissed her all around, then proceeded to the next car." Then, after hitting the Dôme and other cafés of Montparnasse, they crossed over the Seine to the Champs-Élysées, and invaded the Hôtel Claridge, where they "went screaming through the corridors, into the dining room, pulling the noses of the guests, snatching up their drinks, interrupting the dancing, even rushing upstairs to the bedrooms to open whatever doors were not locked to gaze upon the occupants in various states of dress or undress!" Then they proceeded to the actual ball for even more mayhem. The end of the evening found the crowd straggling to the Place de la Concorde, where they washed off their body paint in the fountains there. "It is quite a sight to see several hundred nude bathers of both sexes splashing in the bubbling waters of that famous square."

Not surprisingly, that madcap couple Harry and Caresse Crosby were active participants in the festivities. They hosted a pre-event party at their home at 19 rue de Lille. In his diary from June 18, 1926, Harry told of their costumes (or lack thereof). Caresse "is passionate with bare legs, bare breasts, and a wig of turquoise hair." Meanwhile, Harry was clad in only "a frail red loin-cloth and a necklace of dead pigeons," along with the obligatory red body paint.

That evening, Harry concocted a "tremendous punch (forty bottles of champagne, five whiskey, five gin, five Cointreau)." Amid "mad yells of *Venez Boire* ['come drink'] and then pandemonium and more drinking and more and more" he managed to judge a "most beautiful" contest, which Caresse won "by riding (almost nude) around the ballroom in the jaws of a serpent while myriad students roared approval." By this point, Harry was "ossified" and "sprawled against a pillar," but was "rescued" by a young student named Raymonde. She "was afraid of the mad antics and asked" Harry to "take her home or I her [*sic*] and there was a red blanket and the reek of dead pigeons and then complete oblivion."

☛ **TASTING NOTE:** Although the backstory is a bit preposterous, this is quite a nice drink. It's not often you'll see whiskey and gin together, but they work well here, and the Cointreau balances it out nicely.

I.B.F. PICK-ME-UP

2 ounces brandy
3 dashes Fernet-Branca
3 dashes orange curaçao
3–4 ounces Champagne

Shake the first three ingredients well with ice, then strain into a medium-size wineglass, fill with Champagne.

Recipe from Barflies and Cocktails *(1927), and credited to Bob Card of Harry's New York Bar.*

WITHIN THE VENERABLE INSTITUTION THAT IS HARRY'S New York Bar was the creation of another institution, the International Bar Flies (I.B.F.), essentially a fraternity of legendary Harry's "clients," elbow-benders, and nighthawks par excellence. In *Barflies and Cocktails*, Arthur Moss gave a brief history of "The Birth of the I.B.F." It was the autumn of 1924, when O. O. McIntyre "wrote a mournful article for the *Cosmopolitan*" titled "Beachcombers of the Boulevards," in which he "sorrowfully" referred to the "barflies" of this, "our fair city" of Paris. This prompted the "irrepressible" nightclub owner Jed Kiley to advertise that "the proceeds of Christmas Eve at his Montmartre joint would be donated to the needy barflies of Harry's, Frank's Ritz Bar, and other charitable institutions." This led to Harry MacElhone calling for a meeting of said barflies "at his own urban retreat." Moss made a point to clarify that "Messrs. Kiley and MacElhone" were "genuine philanthropists," and their advertisements shouldn't be interpreted as "business-getters," or anything of a sordid, entrepreneurial nature. Of course not!

So, it came to pass that Christmas of 1924 that "Trap 1" of the I.B.F. was organized at Harry's. The "mellifluous McIntyre" became its "Big Blue Bottlefly" president, "Little Blue Bottlefly" MacElhone its vice president, and "a score of prominent newspapermen were taken in, so to speak, as charter-members." Soon, "the lofty and noble ideals" of the I.B.F. "attracted hordes of intelligent boulevardiers eager for membership," leading to the creation of "associate traps" (chapters) of the I.B.F. As of 1927 Moss reported that "there are over fifty traps and more than five thousand members," in cities ranging from "Shanghai, Liverpool, Madrid, Pittsburgh, Giverny and Warsaw, where members greeted their fellow I.B.F. brethren with a hearty 'fraternal buzz' of 'bzzzzzzzzzzzzz.'"

Like any "secret and sacred fraternal organization devoted to the uplift and downfall of serious drinkers," it had its rules. Rule 4 noted that "those who come to the Trap at 5 A.M. and are able to play a ukulele without a rehearsal are eligible for life membership." Rule 5: "Members bumping their chins on the bar rail in the act of falling are suspended for ten days." Rule 8 reminded Bar Flies that "backslapping after six drinks should be tempered with mercy. Remember, many B.F.s have false teeth." And, Rule 10: "Those sniffling about 'the best little woman in the world' and staying for another round must pay for it."

Moss also listed the first five hundred members of the I.B.F., and a few notable names emerge: McIntyre and MacElhone were numbers 1 and 2, and the third member was none other than Fernand "Pete" Petiot, said to be the inventor of the Bloody Mary. Writer and race track tout Harold Stearns was number 11, Moss number 19, Erskine Gwynne* number 27, George Rehm† number 32, RIP‡ number 33,

---

* See Boulevardier (page 42).

† NPR host Diane Rehm's former father-in-law.

‡ The pen name of Georges Gabriel Thenon, author of *Cocktails de Paris*.

our "old pal"* Sparrow Robertson number 34, Montmartre nightclub owner Joe Zelli number 42, early Hemingway publisher William Bird number 45, and, curiously, way down at number 77, Jed Kiley. Conspicuous by their absences are Ernest Hemingway and F. Scott Fitzgerald, though I suspect they were enshrined in later years.

Also of note, famed novelist Sinclair Lewis was the seventy-second inductee. He was apparently better received at Harry's than he was over on the Left Bank. In addition to a public spat with Harold Stearns described in the following pages, he'd also had a couple of humiliating experiences in Montparnasse. One evening at the Dôme, when he made the mistake of (drunkenly) comparing himself to Gustave Flaubert, he was heckled, "Sit down! You're just a bestseller!"

Where "a tough little flapper" rudely called bestselling author Sinclair Lewis a "withered carrot," the immortal nightclub Le Jockey, 127 boulevard Montparnasse. Now occupied by Chez Fernand. VINTAGE POSTCARD FROM THE AUTHOR'S COLLECTION.

* See My Old Pal (page 146).

McAlmon also recounted a like experience at Le Jockey in 1923. There, a "tough little flapper" called the redheaded Lewis a "withered carrot," and he angrily replied, "Do you know you are speaking to a man of international fame?" When this failed to impress her, Lewis left in a huff.

So while Sinclair Lewis might have been a Barfly at Harry's, he was but a mere gnat in Montparnasse!

☛ **TASTING NOTE:** Perhaps this drink will serve as an introduction to that product you keep hearing about, Fernet-Branca. Fernet is a category of apéritif bitter, Branca is one brand (there are others, such as Ramazzotti, Luxardo, and Cinzano). The Fernet adds a bitter, herbal quality to the brandy base, the curaçao adds sweetness, and the Champagne some effervescence, while also adding volume and drinkability.

SINCLAIR LEWIS, SELF-APPOINTED CRITIC OF THE LEFT BANK

Indeed, not everyone who visited Paris's literary and artistic colony left with a good impression of the state of bohemia. Even a few who lived there could see through some of its phoniness. Perhaps because of his public slightings at the Dôme and Jockey, novelist Sinclair Lewis, bestselling author of *Main Street* (1920) and *Babbitt* (1922), emerged as one of the Dôme's most vocal critics. In an article in H. L. Mencken's *American Mercury*, Lewis attacked the "geniuses and their disciples who frequent the Café du Dôme in Montparnasse," noting further that "all the waiters understand Americanese, so that it is possible for the patrons to be highly expatriate without benefit of Berlitz. It is, in fact, the perfectly standardized place to which standardized rebels flee from the crushing standardization of America."

Lewis's attack zeroed in on Harold Stearns, "father and seer of the Café du Dôme, who is an authority on living without laboring and who bases his opinions of people's intellectual capacity on the amount of money he can borrow off them." Stearns returned fire with both barrels. He called Lewis a "cad, bounder, tightwad, and dumbbell," adding that "he was planning to follow up on his verbal blows by going to America for the special purpose of 'punching Mr. Lewis' face in.'" Stearns also claimed that "if Mr. Lewis himself ever was caught buying a drink for anybody, at least 1,000 people would drop dead."

Not all criticism came from without, however. Ernest Hemingway wrote a scathing piece for the *Toronto Star Weekly* in 1922, calling Paris, "the Mecca of the bluffers and fakers in every line of endeavor." But rather than attack the Dôme, he looked across the street, noting that "you can find anything you are looking for at the Rotonde—except serious artists." He complained further that when tourists visit the Quarter, they mistakenly believe that at the Rotonde "they are seeing an assembly of the great artists of Paris." Au contraire, he noted that its true artists "resent and loathe the Rotonde crowd." He also predicted that these "Rotonders" would scurry back home once "the exchange ever gets back to normal."

Hemingway's sentiments are reminiscent of that classic exchange between Bill Gorton and Jake Barnes in *The Sun Also Rises*, where Bill pretends to chastise Jake (who actually had a job) for being a typical lazy expat. He claimed that Jake had "lost touch with the soil," and that "fake European standards have ruined" him. Bill continued: "You drink yourself to death. You become obsessed by sex. You spend all your time talking, not working. You are an expatriate, see? You hang around cafés." Jake playfully replied, "It sounds like a swell life. When do I work?"

JACK ROSE

1½ ounces applejack or Calvados
¾ ounce gin
¾ ounce fresh orange juice
¾ ounce fresh lemon or lime juice
⅓ ounce dry vermouth
⅓ ounce sweet vermouth
"Grenadine to colour" (about ⅓ ounce)
Lime or lemon peel, for garnish

Shake well with ice, then strain into a chilled cocktail glass. Garnish with twist of lime or lemon peel.

Recipe adapted from Barflies and Cocktails *(1927).*

THE JACK ROSE MAKES TWO APPEARANCES IN ERNEST Hemingway's 1926 novel, *The Sun Also Rises*, one of the quintessential books of the Lost Generation. The story surrounds the dissipated lives of a group of friends in Paris. The protagonist is Jake Barnes, an American journalist living in Paris. Jake is in love with Brett Ashley. Unfortunately, Jake was wounded in World War I, such that he can never consummate his love for Brett.

Chapter VI begins with Jake waiting in vain for her at the Hôtel de Crillon. The previous evening they'd agreed to meet there, however it seems Brett was too drunk to remember it.

The Hôtel de Crillon bar, circa 1920, and the gentleman behind the bar is believed to be immortal "George the barman." PHOTOGRAPH COURTESY OF ART RESOURCE, INC.

At five o'clock I was in the Hotel Crillon, waiting for Brett. She was not there, so I sat down and wrote some letters. They were not very good letters but I hoped their being on Crillon stationery would help them. Brett did not turn up, so about quarter to six I went down to the bar and had a Jack Rose with George the barman.

The Jack Rose and George the barman make another appearance in the novel; Jake's friend Bill Gorton visited George's bar prior to having dinner with Jake. "Stopped at the Crillon," Bill says. "George made me a couple of Jack Roses. George's a great man. Know the secret of his success? Never been daunted." It seems that Bill had more than a couple; in fact, by the time he met up with Jake, he was "pie-eyed."

Both George and the Jack Rose were mentioned in another novel from 1926, that being *Mr. and Mrs. Haddock in Paris, France,* by humorist Donald Ogden Stewart, who happened to be a friend of

Hemingway's.* The book lampoons the typical stodgy, stuffy Americans who ventured over to Europe to have a look around. One scene finds Mr. Haddock at the Ritz Bar, "where he found a great many fine congenial Americans drinking and eating potato chips." One such Yank "seemed to be especially friendly," and offered advice to Haddock. He claimed to have "'seen everything—Luigi's, Ciro's, Zelli's, New York bar, Crillon bar. Seen everything. The best place in Paris to get Jack Rose's [sic] is at the Crillon,' he added. 'Get George to mix them, do you know George? . . . The best bartender in Paris,'" he assured Haddock.

The Jack Rose has a number of interesting "creation theories," that it was named for a New York City gangster ("Bald Jack" Rose), or that its name derives from its similarity in color to the jacqueminot rose, or perhaps, quite simply, that it's an applejack drink with a rose-colored hue. Too much ink has been spilled in the name of deciphering it. The only mystery I'd like to figure out is, what happened to the drink when it crossed over the Atlantic to Paris?

In stateside recipes of the day (and today), the Jack Rose is made with just three ingredients: apple brandy, lemon or lime juice, and a fruit syrup (such as raspberry or grenadine). That's it. It's a simple "sour" cocktail. That's how you'll find it in Hugo Ensslin's *Recipes for Mixed Drinks* (1917) and in *Beverages de Luxe* (1914) by George R. Washburne and Stanley Bronner. But by the time the drink was being made in 1920s Paris, it had taken on a few extra ingredients.† It's as though someone thought it was a fine idea to take the simple Jack Rose and mash it up with the Bronx, because the latter's gin, orange juice, and sweet and dry vermouth were added to the Jack Rose in 1920s Paris. And you know what? It tastes pretty good.

So I wonder if perhaps this version of the Jack Rose is what Jake Barnes was drinking while awaiting his star-crossed lover, Brett. As a

---

* In fact, the hilarious Bill Gorton character in *The Sun Also Rises* was believed to have been based on Stewart's and Hemingway's old friend Bill Smith.

† See *Cocktails* by Piero Grandi (1927); *Barflies and Cocktails* (1927) and *ABC of Mixing Drinks* (1930), both by Harry MacElhone; and *370 Recettes de Cocktails* by Jean Lupoiu (1928).

too-complicated drink for an inextricably tangled relationship, it seems quite fitting to me.

The recipe for the Jack Rose found in *The Artistry of Mixing Drinks* (1936), by the Ritz's head bartender Frank Meier, features the standard three-part format.

☛ **TASTING NOTE:** While the Paris version of this simple drink is a bit more difficult to make, it's worth it. The vermouth offers an aromatic quality much like that of the Presidente, that famous rum cocktail of Cuba. The gin gives it some more backbone and dryness, and the orange juice balances out the tartness. Be careful with the grenadine—don't make it too sweet. Lastly, try the new Laird's Straight Applejack 86—it's superb.

THE REAL LADY BRETT OF
THE SUN ALSO RISES

Hemingway based many of the characters in his 1926 novel, *The Sun Also Rises*, on his friends and acquaintances, much to the dismay of most of them.* Chief among them was Brett Ashley, based on the real-life Lady Duff Twysden. Duff "was undoubtedly the most controversial woman in Montparnasse. She was either loved or despised, and some people went from one attitude to another, but no one appeared to be indifferent or neutral about Duff."

Hadley Hemingway saw her as "a wonderfully attractive Englishwoman, a woman of the world with no sexual inhibitions." Within the novel, "Brett was damned good looking. . . . She was built with

---

* See also "Six Characters in Search of an Author—with a Gun!" (page 74).

curves like the hull of a racing yacht, and you missed none of it with the wool jersey." Of Duff, Hemingway himself noted that "she was not supposed to be beautiful, but in a room with women who were supposed to be beautiful she killed their looks entirely."

Pamplona, July 1926. From left to right: Ernest Hemingway, Harold Loeb, Duff Twysden, Hadley Hemingway, Donald Ogden Stewart, Pat Guthrie. PHOTOGRAPH COURTESY OF THE ERNEST HEMINGWAY COLLECTION, JOHN F. KENNEDY PRESIDENTIAL LIBRARY AND MUSEUM, BOSTON.

Morrill Cody noted, "Like many others, I thought Duff was beautiful, captivating, utterly charming." Socialite Nancy Cunard agreed: "Her shape was lovely, and her figure, the set of her little head, just right, enhanced, as a rule, by a tight-fitting dark blue beret; her thin, well-tailored face, perfect." Humorist Donald Ogden Stewart was equally smitten, noting that Duff "had a kind of style sense that allowed her to wear with dignity and chic almost anything—I mean a man's felt hat, or a matador's hat, maybe even a lampshade."

Some people changed their minds about her. "Both Scott and Zelda Fitzgerald had started out by being very much taken with Duff, but something went wrong, and they both turned bitterly against her, especially Zelda. For a time Zelda and Duff were both queen bees of Montparnasse, and as in the winged world, two queen bees never get along." Duff was present at the Dingo on that fateful day in April 1925 when Hemingway first met F. Scott. She was one of the "worthless characters" that Hemingway was drinking with, and F. Scott later described her and her companion Pat Guthrie as "that girl with the phony title who was so rude and that silly drunk with her."

Dingo bartender Jimmie Charters, who was present when Duff had her first secret meeting with Harold Loeb, said, "She was one of those horsey English girls with her hair cut short in the English manner. Hemingway thought she had class. He used to go dancing with her over on the right bank. I could never see what he saw in her." Robert McAlmon piled on, noting that "of all the various 'ladies' who were on the loose in Paris, she was the most imitated, the least witty or amusing, and she could switch to acting 'her ladyship' at the most dangerous moment."

Speaking of dancing with Hemingway on the Right Bank, nightclub owner Jed Kiley was no Duff fan, either. He recalled an evening when the pair came to his nightclub, Kiley's. "She was awful. Of all the females in the entire world there was only one barred permanently from my place. . . . It was the way she behaved and the way she dressed. . . . And there she was with Hemingway. ⟨She⟩ had used him to crash the gate."

Initially, Kiley's staff wanted to give them "the bum's rush," but Kiley relented. Besides, Hemingway had cleaned up nicely. "He looked pretty good. Almost civilized. He had a *smoking* ⟨jacket⟩ on and was even shaved." Yet Kiley took no chances. He got them "a nice table in the back row behind the post," and he "told her to keep off the dance floor and not bother any of the guests and she could stay this time."

THE JIMMIE SPECIAL

For two people, combine in a cocktail shaker:

1½ ounces Cognac
¾ ounce Pernod
¾ ounce Amer Picon*
¾ ounce mandarin liqueur
¾ ounce cherry brandy
Seltzer water, optional

Shake thoroughly with ice, then strain into highball glasses filled with ice. Drink straight or mix with seltzer water, to taste.

Recipe adapted from Jimmie Charters's autobiography,
This Must Be the Place.

ONE OF THE MOST POPULAR OF THE BARTENDERS OF the day was a Brit named Jimmie "the Barman" Charters, a former boxer from Liverpool. While he worked at many of the bars of the Left Bank, it's perhaps at the Dingo where Jimmie was known best.

Jimmie was a celebrity among the nighthawks of Paris, particularly Montparnasse. His "clients" made up something of a who's who of the literary, artistic, and cultural scene, notably dancer Isadora Duncan, the notorious Kiki,† Lady Duff Twysden, Nancy Cunard,

---

* See the Apéritifs and Liqueurs, Generally chapter (pages 14–68).

† See Kiki Cocktail (page 124).

Jimmie "the Barman" Charters, as shown on the cover of his autobiography. That's the Dingo shown in the lower portion of the cover, formerly at 10 rue Delambre.

British painter Nina Hamnett, former Ziegfeld chorus girl Florence "Flossie" Martin (both Hamnett and Martin were known for their bawdy songs), heiress and patron of the arts Peggy Guggenheim and her husband Laurence Vail, F. Scott and Zelda Fitzgerald, Marcel Duchamp, Harold Stearns, Djuna Barnes, Robert McAlmon, Ford Madox Ford, and Ernest Hemingway (who even wrote the foreword for Charters's memoirs). And when Jimmie moved to a new bartending job, he typically took his following with him.

He worked at many of Paris's legendary watering holes, and his memoirs are full of colorful descriptions and anecdotes from each. He worked at the Imperial, the Trois et As, the Parnasse, the Hôtel de Crillon, Le Jockey, the Jungle, and the Falstaff. Of the Falstaff, Jimmie saw it as "just my type of place, where my personal clients would be well satisfied. . . . The fine part . . . was the atmosphere, which was both gay and churchlike at the same time. The . . . wooden-paneled walls, had a calming effect upon the heavy drinkers, restraining them from too much noise or disorder that might annoy others . . ."

Jimmie might have pined for the Falstaff's calm atmosphere one evening at the Trois et As: it seems there was an English chorus girl who'd had more than a few. She "tore off most of her clothes, and with fists clenched, started to pummel everyone present. Clad only in a pair of lace panties, she was a ridiculous sight, and we all laughed. Angered, she started throwing things, and before she was through I was hiding under the bar." Meanwhile, all of his customers "were in full flight down the rue de Tournon." Alone, she "made herself another drink, sat down at a table, and gently went to sleep!"

Which brings us to the Jimmie Special, which Jimmie invented while he was at the Dingo. See, the drink had its own reputation with the fairer sex. Indeed, this cocktail "had a powerful effect on some of the Quarterites . . . two stiff drinks of it will have some surprising effects! On women this drink had the effect of causing them to undress in public, and it often kept me busy wrapping overcoats around nude ladies!" Even as the drink's reputation spread, women persisted in ordering the Special, and the wild results continued. "I wish I had 100 francs for every nude or semi-nude lady I've wrapped up during the best Montparnasse days!" Alas, eventually "Mrs. Wilson, the wife of the owner of the Dingo, forbade me to make any more Jimmie Specials."

In closing, here's one of Jimmie's favorite jokes of those wild, wicked days of Montparnasse. An English woman with a cockney accent came up to the bar and said, "Give us two w'iskies for two ly-dies." Jimmie, seeing only one woman, politely replied, *"Two* ly-dies? But I don't see but one o' you!" Her reply came quickly: "That's right! That's right! The other ly-dy is restin' in the guttah!"

☛ **TASTING NOTE:** Aside from the salacious backstory, this is actually a pretty good drink. But it does add to its luster when you can offer such a tale, right? While the Jimmie Special's ingredients do require a bit of an investment, it might be the impetus for trying some products that you've never tried and that (fortunately) have a pretty long shelf life. Go easy on the Pernod, as it can overpower the flavor. Napoleon and Cherry Heering are solid choices for the mandarin and cherry liqueur, respectively.

LE JOCKEY

One of the legendary bars that Jimmie Charters helped put on the map was Le Jockey in Montparnasse. Along with Le Boeuf sur le Toit,* it was home to some of the best live jazz you'd find in Paris outside of Montmartre.

Hemingway, who lived just around the corner, described it as "the best night club that ever was . . . best orchestra, best drinks, a wonderful clientele, and the world's most beautiful women." In particular, he remembered its "wonderful jazz, great black musicians who were shut out in the states but welcomed in Paris. . . . Wonderful New Orleans Jazz. Saxophones, horns, drums like I've never heard."

Le Jockey attracted quite an eclectic crowd, including Jane Heap, Mina Loy, Clotilde and Laurence Vail, Robert McAlmon, Mary Reynolds, Man Ray, Harold Van Doren, Jean Cocteau, Jacques Rigaut, Raymond Radiguet, Louis Aragon, René Crevel, Marcel Duchamp—"almost anybody of the writing, painting, musical, gigiloing, whoring, pimping or drinking world was apt to turn up at the

---

* See the Boeuf sur le Toit chapter (page 38).

Jockey," noted McAlmon. It was originally named for and managed by a retired jockey named Miller. It was a big success, but Miller lost a ton of money gambling. The owner hired an unlikely new manager, "Hilaire Hiler, painter, writer, authority on costume, pianist, singer and, suddenly, café manager. Hiler redecorated the Jockey" with his own paintings and murals, which attained international acclaim.

Kiki* was also a fixture at the Jockey, singing "her bawdy songs, delighting patrons with her cheerful vulgarity and sheer joy." Each night, at the close of Paris's theaters, limousines would bring patrons to the Jockey "to drink, talk, and revel in the ongoing party, to the accompaniment of American jazz and blues." Kiki's memoirs recall

In front of Le Jockey, 1923, front row kneeling are left to right: Man Ray, Mina Loy, Tristan Tzara, and Jean Cocteau. Middle row (immediately behind Man Ray): Kiki, an unidentified woman, Jane Heap (in a Russian fur hat), then (probably) Margaret Anderson, and poet Ezra Pound. Back row far left is Bill Bird, an unidentified woman, an unidentified man, "Jockey" Miller (with bow tie, manager of Le Jockey), Les Copeland, Hilaire Hiler, and photographer Curtis Moffat. PHOTOGRAPH COURTESY OF SCALA ARCHIVES.

---

* See Kiki Cocktail (page 124).

that "every night, we're just like one big family there. Everybody drinks a lot, and everybody's happy. Scads of Americans, and what kids they are!"

Hemingway was there one evening with humorist Donald Ogden Stewart and painter Waldo Peirce, "when the place was set on fire by the most sensational woman anybody ever saw. Or ever will. Tall, coffee skin, ebony eyes, legs of paradise, a smile to end all smiles. Very hot night but she was wearing a coat of black fur." It was none other than Josephine Baker. Hemingway claims that they "danced nonstop for the rest of the night." Only at the end of the evening did she reveal that "she had nothing on underneath" her fur coat.

But that wasn't the end of this perhaps apocryphal story. They went back to her place, not for romance but to talk. See, Hemingway was married to Hadley but having an affair with Pauline Pfeiffer. When Hadley learned of the relationship, she directed that Ernest and Pauline must remain apart for one hundred days. If they were still in love after that time, she'd give him a divorce. Long into the night, Hemingway and Baker sat in her kitchen, drinking Champagne, and talked about love, betrayal, guilt, forgiveness, and other matters of the heart. I should note that Hemingway often exaggerated or fabricated stories like this one, so it might contain only a shade of truth, if that. But it's still quite a story!

JUICE OF A FEW FLOWERS

1 ounce London dry gin
1 ounce fresh orange juice
1 ounce grapefruit juice
½ ounce lime juice
½ ounce lemon juice

Shake with ice, then strain into a cocktail glass that has been rimmed with coarse sugar.

Recipe from the Gerald and Sara Murphy archives, courtesy of Laura Donnelly.

ALONG WITH THE BAILEY (PAGE 26), THIS IS ANOTHER invention of Gerald Murphy. He was often secretive about what went into his cocktails; if asked, he might play coy and reply, "Just the juice of a few flowers." Murphy's friend, the playwright Philip Barry, was the author of *The Philadelphia Story*, the 1939 Broadway sensation immortalized on screen in 1940 by Katharine Hepburn, Cary Grant, and James Stewart. He borrowed Murphy's trademark expression for the script. In the scene where Hepburn awakened with a hangover, Grant fixed her a Stinger,* hair of the dog, and all that. Grant suavely explained, "Just the juice of a few flowers. It's a type of stinger. Removes the sting."

Ernest and Hadley Hemingway brought the Murphys to the fiesta of

* See Stinger (page 194).

At a café in Pamplona during the fiesta of San Fermín, 1926. From left to right:
Gerald Murphy, Sara Murphy, Pauline Pfeiffer, Ernest and Hadley Hemingway, and
three shoeshine boys. PHOTOGRAPH COURTESY OF THE ERNEST HEMINGWAY
COLLECTION, JOHN F. KENNEDY PRESIDENTIAL LIBRARY AND MUSEUM, BOSTON.

San Fermín in Pamplona in 1926. Here Hemingway played the instiga-
tor and encouraged a crowd of Spaniards to begin pointing at Sara
and Gerald while chanting, *"Dansa Charleston! Dansa Charleston!"* with
Hemingway leading the crowd in demanding that the couple dance
the hottest dance of the day.* Ultimately, Sara and Gerald obliged.
"They made a circle in the middle of this great big square, and there
Sara and I were. The band started playing jazz. . . . Sara and I stood up
and took hands, with these floodlights on us and all these Spaniards
yelling, and we danced the Charleston. They were delighted."

Later that summer, the Hemingways were also guests at Villa
America. When the Hemingways' young son Bumby came down

---

* According to legend, either Ada "Bricktop" Smith or Josephine Baker brought
the Charleston to Paris.

122 • A DRINKABLE FEAST

with whooping cough, he had to be quarantined. Fortunately, F. Scott Fitzgerald had rented a nearby villa and offered it to the Hemingways. As told by Hadley, the Hemingways, Fitzgeralds, and Murphys still managed to have "happy hour" in spite of the quarantine:

> And all of them would come over yardarm time and sit in their cars outside an iron grille fence and we would be up on this little, tiny porch, and we'd all have drinks together, at a respectable distance, of course. And each empty bottle was put on a spike on the fence, and we really decorated the place in the course of a couple of weeks.

☞ **TASTING NOTE:** Using fresh juices all around makes this drink well worth the effort. If you find the drink a little tart, add a half teaspoon of sugar.

THE VILLA AMERICA, CAP D'ANTIBES, FRANCE

In 1923, having spent a portion of the summer with Cole Porter, Pablo Picasso, and others on the French Riviera, Gerald and Sara Murphy purchased a house on the hillside overlooking Cap d'Antibes. They lovingly restored it and named it Villa America. Dorothy Parker would later call it "the loveliest place in the world."

The house was "in the Moorish style, beige stucco with yellow shutters, and a flagstone terrace, shaded by a linden tree, where the Murphys gave their dinner parties." In the gardens you'd find palms, cedars, and fragrant mimosa and eucalyptus trees. Sara grew her own produce and herbs, and there was an orchard of tangerine, lemon, and olive trees. In addition to a studio for Gerald, "there was an old Provençal farmhouse, which was used for guests." John Dos Passos fondly recalled those magical days:

> It was marvelously quiet under a sky of burning blue. The air smelled of eucalyptus and tomatoes and heliotrope from the garden. I would get up early to work, and about noon walk out to a sand fringed cove named la Garoupe. There I would find the household sunbathing. Gerald would be sweeping the seaweed off the sand under his beach umbrellas. We would swim out through the calm crystal blue water, saltier than salt, to the mouth of the cove and back. Then Gerald would produce cold sherry and Sara would marshal recondite hors d'oeuvres . . .

As writer Donald Ogden Stewart further noted, Gerald and Sara "loved each other, they enjoyed their own company, and they had the gift of making life enchantingly pleasurable for those who were fortunate enough to be their friends." Hemingway described their lifestyle as "that every day should be a fiesta." For Sara, it was very simple: "You loved your friends and wanted to see them every day. . . . It was like a great fair, and everybody was so young."

KIKI COCKTAIL

2 ounces London dry gin
¼ ounce Cointreau
¼ ounce crème de noyaux
2 dashes Angostura aromatic bitters
½ teaspoon simple syrup
½ teaspoon fresh lemon juice
Lemon twist, for garnish

Stir well with ice, then strain into a chilled cocktail glass. Garnish with a lemon twist.

Recipe from Cocktails de Paris *(1929).*

WHILE MUCH HAS BEEN WRITTEN ABOUT THIS DRINK'S namesake, little is known about the drink itself. You'll find it in *Cocktails de Paris* (1929),* and then, curiously enough, in *Boothby's 1934 Reprint World Drinks and How to Mix Them*, published in far-off San Francisco. The drink was named for "Kiki de Montparnasse," née Alice Prin, a peasant girl from Burgundy who came to Paris as a child. She rose from poverty to become not just an artist's model for the likes of Chaïm Soutine, Tsuguharu Foujita, Francis Picabia, Jean Cocteau, Moïse Kisling, and, perhaps most famously, Man Ray, but she also became the undisputed "Queen of Montparnasse." In the

---

* While many of the drinks within this book are attributed to their creator, not so with this one.

foreword he wrote to her memoirs, *The Education of a French Model*, Ernest Hemingway said that "Kiki certainly dominated that era of Montparnasse more than Queen Victoria ever dominated the Victorian era," and that "for about ten years she was about as close as people get nowadays to being a Queen but that, of course, is very different from being a lady."

On any given night during the 1920s, you might find Kiki entertaining at Le Jockey, dancing on the tables at Le Sélect, singing bawdy songs at La Coupole, disrobing on the sidewalk in front of the Dôme and, above all, thoroughly captivating everyone around her. John Glassco noted that "there was no mistaking the magnetism of her personality, the charm of her voice, or the eccentric beauty of her face."

A collection of Montparnasse legends. Back row, second from the left is Louis Wilson, owner of the Dingo (site of photo). Next to him, third from left is bartender Jimmie Charters. The woman seated on the left is Duff Twysden, and on the right is Kiki. PHOTOGRAPH COURTESY OF THE KAY BOYLE PAPERS COLLECTION, SPECIAL COLLECTIONS RESEARCH CENTER, MORRIS LIBRARY, UNIVERSITY OF SOUTHERN ILLINOIS.

Morrill Cody added, "I think it would be more accurate to call her the spirit, the animator of the Quarter. For a number of years, she breathed fire into many gatherings, she stirred the blood of all who knew her, men and women alike." Jimmie Charters described Kiki's popularity as only he could: "I do not suppose there was a singular sailor on the U.S.S. *Pittsburgh* who has not toasted Kiki. Once I saw her on the Dôme terrace with thirty sailors and not another girl!"

A chance encounter in December 1921 changed Kiki's life. Artist and photographer Man Ray was at the Rotonde with painter Marie Vassilieff. There, he noticed two women in a bit of a row. The waiter was refusing them service "because they were not wearing hats. The prettier of the two became irate and shouted that a café was not a church, and besides, 'all the American bitches came in without hats.'" The *patron* (manager) only made matters worse by telling Kiki that "since she was French, the fact that she was sans chapeau and unaccompanied might leave some to mistake her for a whore." At this, Kiki really blew up. Fortunately, Vassilieff knew Kiki and persuaded her and her friend to join them at their table. "The waiter was all apologies—he did not realize that they were Man Ray's friends. And that was how Man Ray met Kiki." They became lovers and she would pose for him in hundreds of photos.

When encouraged to put aside money for the future, Kiki summed up her "live for today" philosophy by responding, "But my dear, I don't give a damn. All I need is an onion, a bit of bread, and a bottle of red; and I will always find someone to offer me that."

☛ **TASTING NOTE:** There's quite an array of flavors here. It's a floral, aromatic, and complex drink. Consider dispensing with the simple syrup and go easy on the crème de noyaux, as they can make the drink too sweet. The orange from the Cointreau and apricot in the noyaux play well together. As for the noyaux, Tempus Fugit or Noyau de Poissy are both fine products.

CAFÉ DE LA ROTONDE, WHERE THE CUSTOMER IS ALWAYS WRONG . . . AND LEAVING

Kiki wasn't the only one who had a bad customer service experience at the Rotonde, and the denizens of Montparnasse were largely ambivalent about the place. Writer Djuna Barnes, for example, found it impossible to actually do any work there: "Everyone just sits around and says 'Gosh, isn't it great to be here!'" Hemingway was no fan; in *The Sun Also Rises* he groused, "No matter what café in Montparnasse you ask a taxi-driver to bring you to from the right bank of the river, they always take you to the Rotonde." He was less subtle in the *Toronto Daily Star.* "The scum of Greenwich Village, New York, has been skimmed off and deposited in large ladles on that section of Paris adjacent to the Café Rotonde." He also called it "the leading Latin Quarter showplace for tourists in search of atmosphere. It is a strange-acting and strange-looking breed that crowd the tables of the Café Rotonde. They have all striven so hard for a careless individuality of clothing that they have achieved a sort of uniformity of eccentricity." He added, "The table-crammed interior of the Rotonde gives the same feeling that hits you as you step into the bird house at the zoo."

Robert McAlmon more succinctly recalled that the Rotonde was "in bad favor with the Americans, for its *patron** was a bastard." Writer Malcolm Cowley apparently shared that sentiment; one evening, he hauled off and punched him. Cowley was arrested but beat the rap in court. Let's just say the prosecution was lackluster—even the police of the Quarter admitted that the *patron* was *mauvais*, or bad.

But it was a similar episode to that endured by Kiki that led to a bit of Montparnasse folklore. It happened one spring morning in 1923, when the *patron* looked out upon the terrace of the Rotonde

---

* "*Patron*" literally means "boss" in French, but in this and other instances herein it means "manager."

Café de la Rotonde, circa 1930.
VINTAGE POSTCARD FROM THE AUTHOR'S COLLECTION.

and observed, to his horror, a pretty young American woman not only hatless, but *smoking*! As Jimmie Charters recalled, "Her hatlessness he might have overlooked, but the smoking—No!" An argument ensued, and other English and Americans at the café sided with the girl. "Finally, the girl rose to her feet and said that if she could not smoke on the terrace she would leave. And leave she did, and she took with her the entire Anglo-American colony!" She crossed the boulevard Montparnasse to the Dôme, and just like that, many of her contemporaries washed their hands of the Rotonde.

But the Rotonde wasn't all *mauvais*, it seems. In another charming piece of Quarter lore, there was the evening when the Rotonde's owner, Victor Libion, attended a party celebrating the artist "⟨Amedeo⟩ Modigliani's sale of a work for several hundred francs." The only problem was that the artist, a Rotonde regular, had basically furnished his flat with items he'd stolen from the café! Indeed, "the chairs, the knives, the glasses, the plates, and even the tables had come from the Rotonde," and when he arrived, Libion instantly recognized all the stolen items. "Soon, he got up and left, and Modigliani berated his friends for bringing him. . . . The party fell silent, when suddenly the door opened and Pére Libion returned, his arms filled with bottles. 'Only the wine wasn't from me,' he told them, 'so I went to get it. Let's go to the table, I am as hungry as a wolf!'"

And, in spite of the Rotonde's rude treatment of Kiki that day, other members of the staff were far kinder. It seems that she had a special friendship with their cooks, "who heated water for her so she could take her bath in the washroom" in the days when she was homeless.

Today's Rotonde is a friendly and stylish place to have a bite to eat or a drink, its "bird house at the zoo" days long behind it.

MANHATTAN

HARRY'S NEW YORK BAR VERSION

2 ounces rye whiskey
1 ounce sweet vermouth
1 dash Angostura aromatic bitters
Cherry, for garnish

Shake well, then strain into a chilled cocktail glass, garnish with a cocktail cherry.

Recipe from ABC of Mixing Cocktails *(1923).*

RITZ BAR VERSION

2 ounces rye whiskey
½ ounce sweet vermouth
½ ounce dry vermouth
1 dash Angostura aromatic bitters
Lemon twist or cherry, for garnish

Stir well, then strain into a chilled cocktail glass, garnish with a lemon twist or cherry.

Recipe from The Artistry of Mixing Drinks *(1936).*

THE MANHATTAN WAS THE DRINK THAT CHANGED THE face of bartending. Invented around 1875, it was the first drink to incorporate a relatively new product, vermouth, into the basic format of the cocktail. Thus, the original whiskey cocktail, made with "spirits of any kind, sugar, water and bitters" (the earliest-known definition of the cocktail, dating back to 1806), became old-school, eventually becoming known as the Old-Fashioned Cocktail. As was summed up nicely in 1898:

> The original cocktails were all made from Gin, Whiskey or Brandy, and these are the spirits used in almost every well-known cocktail made to-day. The addition of Vermouth was the first move toward the blending of cocktails and was the initial feature that led to their popularity.

It was the Manhattan, along with the Martini, that crossed the ocean and helped make cocktails a "thing" around the turn of the past century. More and more "American bars" popped up, especially in London and Paris. Prohibition further enhanced the cocktail's popularity in Europe, as evidenced by this 1921 *Cincinnati Enquirer* item:

> Expelled from their home in the New World, cocktails have met with a hearty welcome in the Old. There they are hailed with general acclaim, for their fame had preceded them. . . . In France, the Manhattan is crowding out the time-honored Apéritif, and it is taken in meditatively, one might always say religiously. The cocktail crystal performs the function of the hour glass in the estaminets of France. A whole hour is devoted to each drink.

Americans traveling abroad in those days still had to be wary of so-called American bars that hadn't a clue about how to make a true cocktail. But as the years went by, the level of proficiency rose. One traveler wrote of his experience at a Paris hotel bar on the rue St. Honoré. He described to the hotel manager his "intense desire for a real Manhattan," and asked if the bartender could make him one. Then, "the bartender placed his hands on the counter, thrust his head forward and said with an unmistakable Bowery accent: "Yah betcher boots he can.""

Then he began tossing into the tumbler the ingredients for two genuine Manhattans. While he was pouring them out, . . . he told us he had been a bartender on the Bowery. Leaving New York for Europe about two years before he had drifted to Paris. . . . We had several Manhattans and then the bartender insisted, Bowery fashion, that we should have "one on the house." These cocktails were the first and only of the real article I had tasted outside of America.

All this said, by the 1920s, guidebooks were still warning the visiting Yanks that they couldn't always count on just any café or bar to serve a good Manhattan. In fact, cocktails in Paris could be seen as a perilous affair. According to *Asbury Park Press* columnist William Ivy, "giving . . . bombs to the baby to play with is less dangerous than entrusting the mild-drinking French with a cocktail shaker."

A final comment on the Manhattan, in *How to Wine and Dine in Paris* (1930), Robert Forrest Wilson warned that:

> In ordering a Manhattan cocktail in Paris, make sure that the barman mixes it with Canadian rye whisky. His ideas about whisky are usually sketchy, and he may use Scotch, which makes an awful mess.

Actually, Mr. Wilson, that makes a Rob Roy.

☞ **TASTING NOTE:** This simple, three-part classic offers many opportunities to experiment, from the types of whiskey, vermouth (or other apéritif wines, such as Byrrh, Dubonnet, or Lillet Rouge), and bitters. Further, pairing a nice spicy rye with Carpano Antica Formula vermouth is a revelation. And by all means, refrigerate and/or decant your vermouth!

MARTINI

1½ ounces London dry gin
1½ ounces dry vermouth
3 dashes Angostura aromatic bitters or orange bitters
Lemon peel, olive, or cherry, for garnish

Stir well with ice, then strain into a chilled cocktail glass. Garnish with lemon peel, olive, or cherry.

Recipe from American Bar: Recettes des Boissons Anglaises & Américaines *(1900).*

MONG THE EXPATS LIVING IN 1920s PARIS, ERNEST Hemingway is likely the one most associated with the Dry Martini. Indeed, he featured it in both of his major novels of the decade. In the final pages of *The Sun Also Rises* (1926), Jake Barnes and Brett Ashley enjoy a couple of Martinis at the Palace Hotel in Madrid, after their adventures in Pamplona. They "sat on high stools at the bar while the barman shook the Martinis in a large nickelled shaker." Once her drink was set before her, "Brett had sipped from the Martini as it stood, on the wood. Then she picked it up. Her hand was steady enough to lift it after that first sip." Having had their cocktails and dinner, Brett remarked, "Oh, Jake, we could have had such a damned good time together," to which Jake sardonically replied, "Isn't it pretty to think so?"

Hemingway also featured the Martini in his 1929 World War I novel, *A Farewell to Arms*. Frederic Henry and his lover, Catherine, are escaping from war-torn Italy into neutral Switzerland. He's gone AWOL and is in civilian attire for the first time in ages. After years of suffering and privations, he longs to feel normal again, and simply wants to reenter civilization. He makes his way to the hotel bar, where he "sat on a high stool and ate salted almonds and potato chips. The martini felt cool and clean. The sandwiches came and I ate three and drank a couple more martinis. I had never tasted anything so cool and clean. They made me feel civilized." The barman tries to talk with him about the war, but Frederic waves him off. "Don't talk about the war," for he'd put it far behind him.

The classic Dry Martini is not a drink you're going to order at just any old bar or restaurant, then or now. A craft cocktail bar? Sure. A good, solid hotel bar? Probably. A shot-and-a-beer bar, sports bar, or the friendly neighborhood pub? Heck no! With the Martini, you choose your spots, and this was also true in 1920s Paris. And that's a bit ironic, because this recipe represents one of the first-ever instances of a Dry Martini* known to cocktail books, and it was published in Paris.

In Paris you had the classic café, the bastion of beers, wines, and apéritifs, favored by the locals. And then you had the so-called American bars, which catered to those more stylish Parisians and the droves of Yanks and Brits coming over on holiday or full-time. American bars flourished like mushrooms. As a whimsical 1921 commentary in the *Duluth News Tribune* explained, "Every hotel in Paree now has an American bar where Tibetan barkeep mixes Egyptian drinks for exiled tourists from Madagascar. It isn't necessary for Americans to speak French in Paris. Your bankroll is your interpreter." The *Washington Evening Star* noted that "there is an American bar at every corner, and Paris offers a martini cocktail without calling it an apéritif." The 1930 guidebook *How to Wine and Dine in Paris*

---

* By "Dry Martini" I mean a Martini made with dry (not sweet) vermouth and London dry (as opposed to the sweeter Old Tom style of gin). Thus, the original Dry Martini was simply a Martini made with drier styles of its components, not necessarily made with more gin and less vermouth, as the term came to imply through the latter part of the twentieth century.

offered a similar observation: "Nowadays one may drink cocktails in Paris and still be Parisian. In fact, to be 'chic' in Paris to-day one must drink cocktails, if anything. It is one of the principal recent changes in the Parisian food-and-drink situation."

In *The Old Waldorf-Astoria Bar Book* (1935), Albert Stevens Crockett observed this phenomenon, noting that "not a few Frenchmen had learned about cocktails in America. The Chatham bar and Henry's and a dozen or more other places knew just how Martinis and Old-Fashioneds were made, and served them. That was one reason why many an American found Paris more enjoyable than London, and stayed longer."

But you had to choose your spots, sound advice coming from *How to Wine and Dine in Paris*: "Ordinarily one in search of a cocktail should take it in an American bar and not order it on a café terrace.... For the barmen in these bourgeois places are apt to have queer ideas about the way to mix a cocktail. However, [Chez] Francis has an

Fellow surrealists Salvador Dalí and Man Ray in Paris.
PHOTOGRAPH COURTESY OF THE US LIBRARY OF CONGRESS, PRINTS AND PHOTOGRAPHS DIVISION, CARL VAN VECHTEN COLLECTION.

136 • A DRINKABLE FEAST

Americanized bar in his café, and you are safe in ordering a Martini there." Indeed, order one in the wrong place and you might suffer the fate of some of the characters in John Dos Passos's 1932 novel, *Nineteen Nineteen*, who "ate in a hurry at Poccardi's and drank a lot of badly made martinis."

So, bottom line, if you were having a Dry Martini or any other true American cocktail in 1920s Paris, you wouldn't have had it in a café or brasserie or bistro, you'd head for the sign that read "American Bar." And as a final note on the Martini, at Harry's New York Bar, they made it with a two-to-one gin-to-vermouth ratio, also with the option of Angostura aromatic or orange bitters, and they *shook* their Martini—they didn't stir it. Perhaps that's why Ian Fleming later pronounced his love for Harry's. As noted in the Americano chapter (page 11), Fleming also adopted the "keep it simple" tack when drinking in a café. Speaking through his James Bond character, in Paris, "if he wanted a solid drink he had it at Harry's bar, both because of the solidity of the drinks and because, on his first ignorant visit to Paris, at the age of sixteen, he had done what Harry's advertisement in the *Continental Daily Mail* had told them to do, and had said to the taxi-driver, *sank roo doe noo* ([*cinq Rue Daunou*]). That had started one of the memorable evenings of his life, culminating in the loss, almost simultaneous, of his virginity and his notecase."

☞ **TASTING NOTE:** As with the Manhattan, please make sure you're using fresh vermouth, and refrigerate or decant those bottles once they're open. When stirring the drink, use twice as much ice as you think necessary, and stir it twice as long. You'll thank me.

SALVADOR DALÍ'S
BLOODY MARTINI

Salvador Dalí came to Paris from Madrid in 1926 and would soon join the growing cadre of Spanish artists, including Pablo Picasso, Joan Miró, Luis Buñuel, and others. And while he loved his double vermouths with olives,* Dalí was also quite the Martini fan. He had his first at the Ritz, in Madrid. Initially, "it tasted horrible to me, but at the end of five minutes it began to feel good inside my spirit." He canceled plans for a haircut and ordered another. But at the bottom of the glass, he noticed "a white hair." While most young men would be devastated, he was euphoric. His mind was a whirl. He became obsessed with that white hair and tried to extract it. "I pressed my finger hard against the glass and slowly pulled it up, slipping it along the crystal with all my might." However, "suddenly a burning pain awakened in" his finger. "I looked, and saw a long cut that was beginning to bleed copiously." He panicked and put his finger back into the glass, "so as not to spatter blood all over my table." Then he saw his error; it wasn't a hair: "It was simply a very fine crack that shone through the liquid of my accursed cocktail. . . . My cocktail became almost instantly colored a bright red and began to rise in the glass."

To this day, you can enjoy a Dalí Martini at the Madrid Ritz, but don't worry, that red tint isn't blood, just a little cherry juice.

* See Vermouth Cocktail (page 221).

MIMOSA

> **4 ounces Champagne or sparkling wine**
> **1–2 ounces fresh orange juice**
>
> ---
>
> "In a large wineglass: a piece of ice, the juice of one-half orange; fill with Champagne, stir and serve."
>
> *Recipe from* The Artistry of Mixing Drinks *(1936).*

A LONG WITH THE BLOODY MARY,* THE MIMOSA IS among the world's most popular breakfast/brunch cocktails. It's also an example of the popularity of orange juice in cocktails from a century ago: witness the Orange Blossom (gin and orange juice), or the Bronx (gin, orange juice, sweet and dry vermouth), and what many believe to be the precursor to the Mimosa, the Buck's Fizz (also orange juice and Champagne, said to have been invented at London's Buck's Club). Credit for the Mimosa generally goes to Frank Meier, and his 1936 recipe is shown above. Frank was the head bartender from the opening of the Ritz Bar in 1921, until after World War II (circa 1947).

Frank alternatively called the drink the Champagne Orange, and we see references to it as early as 1923. In his diary entry from August 25, Harry Crosby wrote:

Geraldine and champagne orangeades at the Ritz and afterwards to dance in the Bois and to dance in the Montmartre and finally at dawn

---

* See Bloody Mary (page 34).

to Les Halles where we were the only two dancers. Seven o'clock and the end of the last bottle of champagne and a crazy bargain with a sturdy peasant to haul us to the Ritz in his vegetable cart . . . upon the heaped-up carrots and cabbages while our poor man strained in the harness . . .

But wait, there's more. Harry Crosby's diary from August 29, 1923, tells us of the tortuous ennui that can be suffered only by a wealthy playboy who "works" for his billionaire uncle J. P. Morgan's bank in 1920s Paris:

I feel so lifeless, haven't even the courage to go out in the canoe, too weary to work at stocks and bonds or even to read the Bible. All I am good for is to drink champagne orangeades with Geraldine in the garden of the Ritz, the only oasis in the stagnant August Paris.

☞ **TASTING NOTE:** Also like the Bloody Mary, the Mimosa can be personalized or embellished. In some recipes, Grand Marnier is added, and many believe this to be the original formula, though it's not found in Meier's 1936 recipe.

MANY A WILD MONTMARTRE NIGHT IN *LES ANNÉES FOLLES** ENDED AT LES HALLES

Having read a fair amount of memoirs and guidebooks from 1920s Paris, Harry Crosby's Ritz-to-Bois-to–Les Halles spree sounds almost like your typical night. To translate, it seems that Harry and a woman (not his wife) named Geraldine had Mimosas at the Ritz, then danced the night away in the Bois (a beautiful park in the west of Paris with a number of chic restaurants and clubs, notably the Château de Madrid, Hôtel Armenonville, Les Cascades, and Le Pré Catelan), then on to Montmartre for more dancing, then at 7:00 a.m., having consumed an ocean of Champagne, they made their way to Les Halles.

Remember back in college when, after a big night, you'd end up at that greasy-spoon diner for breakfast or cheese fries? This was Les Halles, at least to overnight revelers in *les années folles*, where they'd go for *la soupe a l'oignon*—what we bourgeoise Americans would call French onion soup. Les Halles was "the great market place of Paris. At crack of Dawn, hundreds of hucksters open up their vegetable and fruit stands right out on the street and begin to do business." Where might you go for your *soupe a l'oignon* fix? The popular night-owl destination at Les Halles was a place called Au Père Tranquille, vividly described in 1927's *Paris with the Lid Lifted*:

> This, a quaint workingman's café. In the center of the market. You go upstairs. The hucksters eat downstairs. A funny little orchestra. You can dance or sing. Other "slummers" all around you, in evening dress . . . They are out to see it all, too. And, oh, how they hate that onion soup."

* Translated to "the crazy years."

LES HALLES " AU PÈRE TRANOUILLE " SOUPERS

Late-night "slummers" outside Au Père Tranquille, adjacent to the great
markets of Les Halles and famous for its French onion soup.
VINTAGE POSTCARD FROM THE AUTHOR'S COLLECTION.

So Harry Crosby was only doing what the guidebook *Paris on Parade* (1930) would consider de rigueur a full year later, which told readers: "It has therefore become the fashion with the frivolous after a night spent with the gaieties and champagne of Montmartre to repair to Les Halles at dawn for *la soupe a l'oignon*." Check.

American expat Robert McAlmon had a similarly epic night during that very same summer of 1923. After an evening in Montmartre, he ran into Hilaire Hiler and Wynn Holcomb. "Boys, what we need is a drink," said Holcomb. For McAlmon, it was pretty late, a long night of imbibing already behind him. "I was drinking gin now," he noted, "having drunk myself into a second or third soberness." After a few Cognacs, Hiler and Holcomb retired, to be replaced by Kenneth Adams.

On their winding, wobbly way to Les Halles, "at every bistro we stopped to have another Cognac." Before too long, McAlmon and

Adams were "hailed by two street girls," who joined the party. Finally ending up at Les Halles, the two gents "agreed to buy them coffee and croissants, while we had *soupe à l'oignon.*"

And as for Crosby's wagon ride from Les Halles back to the Ritz? None other than F. Scott Fitzgerald might shrug and say, "Been there, done that." Indeed, a short story fragment he later repurposed in *Tender Is the Night* went something like this:

> Then six of us, oh, the best the noblest relics of the evening . . . were riding on top of thousands of carrots in a market wagon, the carrots smelling fragrant and sweet with earth in their beards—riding through the darkness to the Ritz Hotel and in and through the lobby . . . and the bought concierge had gone for a waiter for breakfast and champagne.

MONKEY GLAND

1½ ounces London dry gin
1½ ounces fresh orange juice
1 teaspoon grenadine
1 dash absinthe

Shake well with ice, then strain into a chilled cocktail glass or coupe.

Recipe from ABC of Mixing Cocktails *(1923), which includes the comment, "invented by the author, and deriving its name from Voronoff's experiments in rejuvenation."*

THIS DRINK'S NAME COMES FROM THE LIFE'S WORK OF Dr. Serge Voronoff. His career was dedicated to the theory that the sex glands of living organisms hold the key to health, vigor, and drive. This is from his 1920 manifesto:

> The sex gland stimulates cerebral activity as well as muscular energy and amorous passion. It pours into the stream of the blood a species of vital fluid which restores the energy of all the cells, and spreads happiness, and a feeling of well-being and the plentitude of life throughout our organism. . . . The idea of capturing this marvelous force . . . had haunted my mind for a number of years . . .

I'm assuming you're sitting down, since we're veering into real "mad scientist" territory here.

Voronoff embarked on a series of celebrated experiments, in which he grafted the testicles of monkeys onto his human subjects, and initially reported Fountain of Youth–like results. By 1927, he claimed that he'd successfully performed more than one thousand procedures, which would yield "a life span of 125 years and an old age of a few months." Alas, as the 1930s wore on, growing skepticism surrounded his methods, and by World War II he was largely discredited. He died in 1951, still holding on to the dream.

By 1919, reports coming out of Britain told of a host of new cocktails being offered by London's finest bartenders. News of one such drink was trumpeted in a widely syndicated *New York Times* story straight from London. "'MONKEY GLAND' LATEST COCKTAIL," screamed the headline. "The 'monkey gland' cocktail has arrived. Orange juice, gin and a dash of absinthe are the principal ingredients." By 1923, the drink had taken Paris by storm, according to a June 7 story in the *Schenectady Gazette*, the headline of which blared "'MONKEY GLAND' IS POPULAR IN PARIS."

Popular culture being what it is, Voronoff's practices found their way into more things than just cocktails. Indeed, in the Marx Brothers' 1929 film, *The Cocoanuts* [sic], there's a little ditty, penned by Irving Berlin, no less, called "The Monkey Doodle Doo," which contains the following priceless lines:

> *Let me take you by the hand over to the jungle band.*
> *If you're too old for dancing, get yourself a monkey gland,*
> *And then let's go—my little dearie, there's the Darwin theory,*
> *Telling me and you to do the Monkey Doodle Doo.*

Even poet E. E. Cummings got in on the act; his poem "XVIII," from his 1926 collection, *is 5*, contains a reference to the "famous doctor" who "inserts monkeyglands [sic] in millionaires," referring to it as "a cute idea n'est-ce pas?"

Not to be outdone, French bartender Jean Lupoiu offered his own take, in his 1928 book, *370 Recettes de Cocktails*:

VORONOFF COCKTAIL

¾ ounce vodka
¾ ounce Martinique rhum
³/₈ ounce Zubofka *
³/₈ ounce Scotch whisky

And the "Cocktails Round Town" portion of *Barflies and Cocktails* contained another spoof, invented by a fellow named W. C. Weaver. "The wintergreen Weaver says it's good for all young boys over forty-five like 'Sparrow' or George Bowles." Here's how:

STIFFERINO COCKTAIL

1 ounce Fernet-Branca
1 ounce Cinzano sweet vermouth
1 ounce Noilly Prat dry vermouth
1 dash brandy

Drink this, the recipe avows, "and Methusaleh would think he was Ponce de Leon."

☛ **TASTING NOTE:** The Monkey Gland is an acquired taste. It's basically an Orange Blossom (page 149) with a little absinthe and grenadine. If you find the absinthe overpowering, you can cut it back.

---

* "Zubofka" likely refers to Żubrówka, a category of neutral spirit flavored with bison grass, dating back to sixteenth-century Russia, Poland, and Belarus. While there is a brand of vodka on the market today bearing that name, it is an approximation of the original style, as bison grass is illegal in the United States.

MY OLD PAL

1 ounce rye whiskey (the original recipe called
for Canadian Club)
1 ounce dry vermouth (or possibly sweet—see page 148)
1 ounce Campari
Orange peel, for garnish

Add all ingredients to a mixing glass filled with ice. Stir well, then strain into a rocks glass filled with fresh ice. Garnish with an orange peel.

Recipe from Barflies and Cocktails *(1927).*

THIS DRINK IS OFTEN THOUGHT OF AS THE RYE WHISKEY version of the Boulevardier (page 42), which of course is the Bourbon version of the Negroni, which naturally is the gin version of the Americano (page 11) . . . I'll stop there.

Often shortened to just the "Old Pal," this drink likely made its debut in the "Cocktails Round Town" portion of *Barflies and Cocktails* (1927). Within those pages, Arthur Moss recalled that "way back in 1878, on the 30th of February to be exact," his "old pal 'Sparrow' Robertson" said to him, "Here's the drink I invented when I fired the pistol the first time at the old Powderhall foot races and you can't go wrong if you put a bet down on 1/3 Canadian Club, 1/3 Eyetalian Vermouth, and 1/3 Campari."

Moss further explained that Sparrow would "dedicate this cocktail to me and call it, My Old Pal."*

About that vermouth, in years past, country names were used to identify vermouth. Italian meant "sweet," and French meant "dry." So why would I give you this recipe, calling for dry vermouth, when the 1927 recipe listed "Eyetalian"? Well, the recipe in the 1929 and later editions of MacElhone's other cocktail book, *ABC of Mixing Cocktails*, called for French vermouth, meaning dry, so it's assumed he was correcting a mistake in his 1927 book. But in the end, they're both good drinks.

So who was this Sparrow Robertson? His 1941 obituary described him as "the most remarkable columnist of them all—the *Paris Herald*'s cocky, antique, legend-crusted, peewee . . . universally known as the Sparrow." Born in Scotland, William "Sparrow" Robertson was raised and spent the early part of his career in New York City. He was active in officiating sporting events, and ran a sporting goods store (or was it a saloon?) called the Sparrow's Nest in lower Manhattan. In 1914, "Sparrow came to France to win the war. Too old for service, he was hired by the Knights of Columbus to help with athletic events" for US personnel. According to columnist Damon Runyon, he took a look around him and inquired, "'How long has this been going on?' He has been in Paris, France, ever since." He somehow wrangled a position with the Paris edition of the *New York Herald*, though there was "no evidence that he had ever written a line of newspaper copy." Sparrow spent the rest of his career as the *Herald*'s sporting editor (more gossip than sports), and he soon became one of the City of Light's most prodigious night owls. Perhaps one of his favorite drinks, which he called "drenched" coffee (coffee spiked with applejack), helped to keep him awake all those hours.

His obituary noted that "his headquarters were the 'thirst emporiums' on the Right Bank," likely referring to the favorite watering holes of writers and newspapermen, notably Henry's, the Hôtel Chatham bar, Les Caves Murae, Vetzel's, and, of course, Harry's New York Bar. Sadly, only Harry's remains to this day. Whenever Sparrow

---

* See also Boulevardier for more on Moss, page 42.

learned of a colleague's imminent departure from Paris, he'd organize a "death watch," to stay up with that fellow all night, for fear he might oversleep and miss his train. Or perhaps having the old pal miss that train was the whole point, who knows? Then, Sparrow would somehow write that day's "column on the night's adventures. It was a unique column—a syntax-slaughtering chronicle which editors were carefully warned not to unscramble."

Sparrow wasn't the only nighthawk in the family. His wife was known to do a bit of clubbing herself, evidenced by an ad Sparrow felt compelled to run in the *Paris Tribune* on New Year's Day 1925, which read: "My wife having left my bed and board I will not be responsible for any bills run up at Kiley's," a popular Montmartre nightclub.

About that nickname, Ring Lardner described him as "five foot one with a sparrow's chest," and the nickname was from his early days in Manhattan. Back in the 1870s, Sparrow was attending a Tammany Club dance in "a rented dress suit many times too large" when someone inquired, "Who is the Sparrow?" It stuck; in fact, he later made it his legal name. And perhaps because of his slight frame, "Sparrow spoke always out of the side of his mouth as though he were a toughie."

As an aside, you can disregard the "way back in 1878, on the 30th of February" nonsense as an inside joke. Moss was born in 1889, and even in a leap year no February ever had thirty days. Further, Robertson was known for joking that his autobiography would start with "I remember one time, shortly after the battle of Gettysburg . . ."

☞ **TASTING NOTE:** Like the Americano, Boulevardier, and Negroni variations, feel free to swap out different styles of vermouth or apéritif bitters, or perhaps see if you prefer it up or on the rocks.

ORANGE BLOSSOM

2 ounces London dry gin
Juice of one orange (approximately 2 ounces)

Shake well with ice, then strain into a chilled cocktail glass or coupe.

Recipe from Barflies and Cocktails *(1927).*

THE MAKEUP OF THIS DRINK OFTEN DEPENDS ON WHEN and where you're finding it. It's typically thought of as a Prohibition drink, with orange juice masking that nasty bathtub gin. But before the Volstead Act, you'd find it being fancied up with the addition of sweet vermouth (see the 1906 *Louis' Mixed Drinks* by Louis Muckensturm), and both sweet and dry vermouth (as in the 1914 *Beverages de Luxe* by George R. Washburne and Stanley Bronner). Yet "American bars" in 1920s Paris were serving the Prohibition model, which is a little surprising, as the local bartenders tended to add vermouth to drinks not typically having it, witness the Jack Rose and the Bacardi Cocktail. But there you are. Perhaps they were catering to the visiting Americans fleeing Prohibition.

The Orange Blossom was a favorite of both F. Scott and Zelda Fitzgerald, and was "Zelda's cocktail of choice." So much so that their summer of 1920 became "a summer of a thousand giant orange blossoms, with their biggest household expense the bootlegger." And I'm guessing that many of those oranges being juiced each weekend in Fitzgerald's 1925 novel, *The Great Gatsby*, were going into Orange Blossoms. And then there was the time that Zelda and a friend drank an entire pitcher, then packed some in a thermos for a round of golf at the country club, where they "became drunk on the course, with Zelda singing, '"You can throw a silver dollar down upon the ground, and it will roll, because it's round."'" Fitzgerald friend Ring Lardner (who had a thing for Zelda, by the way) escorted them home safely.

As an aside, Lardner visited the Fitzgeralds in Saint-Raphaël on the Riviera in 1924. In a subsequent magazine article, Lardner playfully described the couple as "Mr. Fitzgerald is a novelist and Mrs. Fitzgerald is a novelty." He explained that F. Scott and Zelda had moved from New York to France "because New Yorkers kept mistaking their Long Island home for a road house." Lardner didn't arrive empty-handed; "I made Mr. Fitzgerald a present of some rare perfume that said Johnnie Walker on the outside of it which I had picked up at Marseilles. It was coals to Newcastle, so I took it back to the hotel."

Getting back to the drink, it seems the combination of gin and orange juice eventually wore thin. In 1934, both the Orange Blossom and the Bronx made *Esquire* magazine's "Ten Worst Cocktails" list. Further, G. Selmer Fougner, in his *New York Sun* "Along the Wine Trail" column, speculated that because "everyone had gin, everyone had orange juice, and by the 1930s everyone was sick of the combination."

The Orange Blossom was also the first drink ever enjoyed by Robert Benchley, and he waited thirty-two years for his first one! An avowed teetotaler, his friends told him he should sample alcohol before condemning it, so he finally relented. He took one sip of his Orange Blossom, turned to Dorothy Parker, and said, "This place should be closed down." After getting that out of his system, he finished it and ordered another.

☛ **TASTING NOTE:** If you're having another yourself, do try some of the earlier recipes, as discussed on page 150. It really becomes a more sophisticated cocktail with the inclusion of vermouth.

CROSSING THE ATLANTIC
WITH DOTTIE AND BOB

In February 1926, Ernest Hemingway went to New York to sign a contract with Scribner's to publish *The Sun Also Rises*, including a whopping $1,500 advance. Now it was time to celebrate. He spent several days in New York, and met "hells own amount of people," notably Robert Benchley and Dorothy Parker. Somehow during those raucous few days he convinced Bob and Dottie to join him on his cruise back to Paris. And that's what they did.

On the day of their departure on the SS *President Roosevelt*, Hemingway "stopped at several bootleggers en route to Hoboken." After all, he couldn't cross the Atlantic without a good supply of booze. Meanwhile, Parker brought "a week's supply of scotch" of her own. After a jovial bon voyage party, they departed New York Harbor amid a raging blizzard. Parker might have wanted that Scotch to calm her nerves; after all, her aunt and uncle, Lizzie and Martin Rothschild, had been aboard the *Titanic* that fateful night in 1912, and Martin was among the dead.

The following morning, Parker "woke up to a tragedy infinitely worse than a shipwreck. Her stash of Scotch had been stolen, a catastrophe she blamed on the bon voyage revelers, most likely her Rothschild and Droste relatives." Things got worse for Benchley, too. According to Hemingway, Benchley had trouble getting a stateroom, so the *Roosevelt* simply "put him anywhere there was and there wasn't anywhere so he slept in one of the maid's rooms and the 4th day out he said it was funny but he felt just like the time he had crabs and the 6th day out he had crabs."

Somehow, Dottie and Bob managed to have a good visit to France, and were among the frequent guests that summer at the Villa America. But that trip across on the *Roosevelt* was forgettable.

PERNOD COCKTAIL

> **2 ounces Pernod**
> **½ ounce water**
> **1 dash Angostura aromatic bitters**
> **¼ teaspoon sugar**
>
> ---
>
> Shake well with ice, then strain into a chilled cocktail glass.

TO UNDERSTAND PERNOD YOU SHOULD FIRST UNDERSTAND absinthe. Prior to World War I, absinthe was the most popular distilled spirit in France, but when it was banned,* it left quite a void. The French government eventually allowed the manufacture of an anise-based spirit (*anis*, in French), but without wormwood. By 1923, you'd find an 80-proof "Anis Pernod" offered by the Jules Pernod family, and that firm would merge with Pernod Fils to relaunch the brand. Pernod became a popular absinthe substitute, and spawned many imitators, becoming as ubiquitous as the absinthe they replaced.

It's important to understand the distinctions between absinthe, anise, and anisette, not to mention pastis. To most people, the terms are used interchangeably, because they all taste more or less like licorice. Absinthe is a distilled spirit with star anise as the principle flavor but also contains fennel, coriander, hyssop, and veronica. It has no added sugar and is relatively high-proof (40–50 percent alcohol). Anise is simply wormwood-free absinthe, and similarly has no

---

* See Absinthe (page 3).

added sugar and is also higher proof. Pernod is an example. Anisette, meanwhile, is a liqueur, not a spirit. It is lower proof and has added sugar, and its flavoring is mainly from star anise. Finally, pastis (the first, Ricard, debuted in 1932) is another absinthe substitute; it's also a spirit (not a liqueur) and is similar in flavor, but in addition to anise, it also contains licorice root.

The 1930 guidebook *How to Wine and Dine in Paris* explained the popularity of anise:

> But France since the Armistice has discovered a substitute for absinthe which may account for the complete success of the prohibition law. . . . Its manufacture is getting to be a tremendous business in France. . . . A dozen anise brands are on the market, and new ones appear constantly. . . . The anise *apéritifs* are extremely powerful, and those who have sampled them testify to a dreamy effect from them— a fact which gives rise to a popular but perhaps erroneous belief that they contain some of the narcotic principles which led to the banishment of absinthe. At the *apéritif* hour in Paris you see more Frenchmen in the cafés drinking anise than any other alcoholic beverage except beer.

The *Asbury Park Press* added that "these new decoctions . . . have all the qualities of absinthe except the prohibited poison. They taste like it, and they become cloudy when mixed with water. They also have a powerful kick. After two of them, one has a tendency to forget important business appointments."

Bartender Jimmie Charters also observed a "when in Rome" effect, that "new arrivals from England or America almost always started on Pernod." Indeed, when a newbie encountered "a number of dignified old gents sitting on the café terrace drinking this milky liquid with the entrancing color," he says, "I will try one." Sadly, Jimmie observed that while the average Parisian had just one, before a meal, "the Englishman drinks one after another, quietly but steadily, while the American gulps his down. Well, they both learn! At the end of a month most of them switch to something milder, usually cocktails, fizzes, or other fancy drinks." Jimmie also noted that because of Pernod's strength and cloudy white color, "the French workmen called it *lait de tigre*—tiger's milk!"

Montparnasse nightclub owner Jed Kiley saw Pernod as the official drink of the would-be writer: "They sat around the Dôme drinking fines and Pernods and wrote books about Paris. Then you never heard about them again."

You'll find Pernod in Ernest Hemingway's 1926 novel, *The Sun Also Rises*. In Chapter III, Jake is having an apéritif in the early evening. It's "a warm spring night," and he's sitting "on the terrace of the Napolitain, . . . watching it get dark and the electric signs come on, and the red and green stop-and-go traffic-signal, and the crowd going by . . ." He catches the eye of a passing *poule*, a polite term for a prostitute, and she joins him. As she orders a Pernod, Jake playfully warns her, "That's not good for little girls." Smartly, she replies, "Little girl yourself," and then to the waiter, "*Dites garçon, un pernod.*" Jake, as narrator, explains that "Pernod is a greenish imitation absinthe. When you add water, it turns milky. It tastes like licorice and it has a good uplift, but it drops you just as far. We sat and drank it and the girl looked sullen."

In another scene, Jake and Bill Gorton went on an evening walk before dinner, and Jake notes that Bill is "about a hundred and forty-four" drinks ahead of him. Indeed, Bill is "pie-eyed"; he'd already had a few of George the barman's Jack Roses at the Crillon. "George's a great man," Bill exclaims. "Know the secret of his success? Never been daunted." Jake replies, "You'll be daunted after about three more Pernods."

Pernod is also in Henry Miller's controversial novel *Tropic of Cancer*: "When we get out of the taxi in front of her hotel he's trembling so much that I have to walk him around the block first. He's already had two Pernods, but they haven't made the slightest impression on him." And, echoing the perhaps misogynistic theme that Pernod is a man's drink, Jean Rhys has Pernod in her semiautobiographical 1928 novel, *Quartet* (based on her affair with mentor Ford Madox Ford):

When the lonely night came it started hurting like hell. Then she would drink a couple of Pernods at Boots's Bar to deaden the hurt. . . .

"A Pernod fils, please."

"Pernod is very bad for the stomach, mademoiselle," the patronne said disapprovingly. "If mademoiselle had a Dubonnet instead?"

The patronne was really a wonderfully good sort. Fancy caring what happened to the stomach of a stray client. On the other hand, fancy facing life . . . on a Dubonnet! Marya could have cackled with laughter.

"No, a Pernod," she insisted. And a minute afterwards the merciful stuff clouded her brain.

I should note that this recipe is just one of the ways in which Pernod was (and is) enjoyed in Paris. For most folks it's too strong to drink straight, and is "meant to be diluted"; the standard ratio is four to five parts water to one part Pernod. A little sugar is often added, too. Pernod is strong stuff, and drinking it straight might be a bit, shall we say, daunting.

☞ **TASTING NOTE:** Perhaps this is the drink that leads you to appreciate the more complex flavors and potency of dripped absinthe, as the water and the sugar make it a more accessible drink.

PIERRE LOVING'S PET PUNCH

1½ ounces Cinzano bitters or Campari
¾ ounce sweet vermouth
¾ ounce Port
³/₈ ounce grenadine
³/₈ ounce rum
Lemon peel, for garnish (optional)

Stir all ingredients well with ice, then strain into a chilled cocktail glass. No garnish called for, but a lemon peel works well.

Recipe adapted from Barflies and Cocktails *(1927).*

THIS IS YET ANOTHER DRINK FROM ARTHUR MOSS'S "Cocktails Round Town" segment of *Barflies and Cocktails*, where Moss offered the favorite libations of notable "Barflies" buzzing 'round Harry's New York Bar. The drink's description simply reads, "Pierre Loving pauses a minute in his labor of chronicling the Latin Quarter to explain the mysteries of his own pet punch." After giving the recipe, the item concludes, "That's the punch that's the life, and death, of the studio party."

I cannot help but be struck by the choice of words; it's as if Moss were clairvoyant. Allow me to explain. Pierre Loving was a poet, writer, and journalist, notably of the Paris edition of the *New York*

Herald, which also employed "Sparrow" Robertson.* It was Pierre Loving's reporting on a more literal punch that stoked the ire of another writer in Paris, that being Ernest Hemingway.

Hemingway was quite the boxing enthusiast. He would often spar with his mentor, Ezra Pound, in exchange for Pound's tutelage. When former *Toronto Daily Star* colleague Morley Callaghan moved to Paris in 1929, he and Hemingway would spar at the American Club and then repair to the Sélect for a drink or two. Occasionally, they would box three-minute rounds, requiring a timekeeper. One time, it was Spanish painter Joan Miró, if you can believe that. According to Callaghan, "Miró added a touch of solemn Spanish dignity to the affair." But another time, the timekeeper was none other than F. Scott Fitzgerald.

It seems that during the second round, F. Scott got distracted and lost track of time. "Scott had none of Miró's high professionalism," Callaghan recalled. "He was too enchanted at being there with us." The opening round was uneventful, each boxer feeling the other out. But in the second round, "Ernest got careless," and Callaghan took advantage, landing a haymaker to Hemingway's jaw. Down went Hemingway, "sprawled out on his back."

> "Oh, my God!" Scott cried suddenly. . . . "I let the round go four minutes!"
>
> "Christ!" Ernest yelled, then growled savagely. "All right, Scott, . . . if you want to see me getting the shit knocked out of me, just say so. Only don't say you made a mistake."

Hemingway was full of excuses as to why he was bested. It was a heavy prefight lunch with F. Scott at Prunier's, or that "I couldn't see him hardly—*had a couple of whiskeys en route*." Nevertheless, that was the last boxing match between Hemingway and Callaghan.

Suffice it to say, this incident caused some harm to their friendships, but it didn't end there, and that's where Pierre Loving comes in. See, when Loving heard about the affair, he "belatedly sent a

---

* See My Old Pal (page 146).

distorted version of the story to the *Denver Post*." This led to a snarky story in the *New York Herald Tribune*, in which Isabel Paterson reported that after Hemingway and Callaghan had had an argument at the Café du Dôme, "Callaghan knocked Hemingway out cold." The tale grew more twisted from there, with the parties demanding retractions, apologies being issued, attempts made at calming the waters, et cetera. "All was (more or less) forgiven when a correction finally appeared on December 8. But Hemingway would never forgive Pierre Loving."

So, here you have Arthur Moss, in a 1927 cocktail book, offering a Pierre Loving's Pet Punch, a "punch that's the life, and death, of the studio party." As it happened, Loving's indiscreet reporting of a different variety of punch brought a great deal of life, and death, to the 1929 boxing parties of Messrs. Hemingway and Callaghan. You cannot make this stuff up!

☛ **TASTING NOTE:** This is quite an interesting drink and can take on many expressions depending on your choice of rum (Plantation Rum Guadeloupe 1998 is superb), as well as the sweetness of the Port. For additional character, try a funky rhum agricole, or a dark Jamaican. The Port marries beautifully with the rum, offering chocolate and toffee notes. And you've probably never seen this color in a drink before.

HEMINGWAY AND MIRÓ

Four years earlier, Hemingway purchased Miró's now-famous painting *The Farm* for 3,500 francs (about $166 at the time, though some reports have it as 5,000 francs, and $250) as a birthday present for Hadley. Originally, Hemingway's friend and poet Evan Shipman had arranged to purchase it, but when he learned of Ernest's love for the painting, he said, "Hem, you should have *The Farm*. I do not love anything as much as you care for that picture and you should have it." But in order to make the final payment, Hemingway, Shipman, and John Dos Passos had to go from café to bar, borrowing money. Traveling back to Hemingway's apartment, "In the open taxi the wind caught the big canvas as though it were a sail, and we made the taxi driver crawl along."

Hemingway later said the painting "has in it all that you feel about Spain when you are there and all that you feel when you are away and cannot go there," and further, "no one could look at it and not know it had been painted by a great painter." It now hangs in the National Gallery of Art in Washington, DC, and Hemingway's savvy purchase is now worth many millions of dollars.

QUARTIER LATIN COCKTAIL

2 ounces Dubonnet

1 ounce Amer Picon*

1 teaspoon Cointreau

Shake well, then strain into a chilled cocktail glass.

Recipe from ABC of Mixing Cocktails *(1930).*

THIS DRINK FIRST APPEARS IN THE 1923 BOOK *ABC OF Mixing Cocktails*, in which the recipe is credited to a Dick Garrick. However, the 1930 edition of the same book states, "Recipe by Wilson's Dingo Bar, Rue Delambre, Paris." Perhaps Garrick was a Dingo barman.

Technically speaking, the term "Quartier Latin" (Latin Quarter) refers to that part of the Left Bank surrounding the intersection of boulevards Saint-Germain and Saint-Michel, home to the Sorbonne and other schools, the name likely due to Latin being the classical language of higher learning. But when you're reading about 1920s Paris and its expat colony, the term "Quarter" can take on a broader meaning, as it will include other Left Bank neighborhoods, notably Montparnasse. It's like how New Yorkers today might generally refer to the Village when really they're in nearby Chelsea or SoHo.

Along with the Jimmie Special (page 114), this is another of the

---

* See the Apéritifs and Liqueurs, Generally chapter (page 14).

drinks invented at the Dingo Bar (10 rue Delambre, now an Italian restaurant, Auberge de Venise). Along with the Dôme, the Rotonde, La Coupole, the Sélect, the Jockey, the Falstaff, Pirelli's/the College Inn, the Parnasse, the Stryx, the Jungle, and Closerie des Lilas and a few others, the Dingo was one of the legendary watering holes of 1920s Montparnasse. Here, in the afternoon, evening, and long into the night, expats would meet, talk, solve the problems of the world, and, of course, drink. After all, to quote the Dingo's bartender, Jimmie Charters, "Talk is a great encouragement to drinking, and there has never been any lack of that in Montparnasse." They'd migrate from this bar to that café, like legendary barfly Robert McAlmon, "always seeking another name, and another face, in quite another place." Why? Because McAlmon would say, "There is a Paris full of people I have to have a drink with yet."

Prior to 1923, the Dingo had been an ordinary bistro, its clientele mainly French working class. As Montparnasse became an Anglo-American colony, the owner (a Frenchman named Harrow) redecorated it, installed an American bar and an English-speaking bartender. A 1925 newspaper account noted that the "Dingo was conceived about a year ago for Americans who had invaded the quarter in great numbers and it developed quickly into the only place on the Left Bank where satisfactory old-fashioned American cocktails could be had. Mike, a French-Canadian from Quebec, the bar tender, has been written into the quarter's history to mix with the shades of Voltaire, Verlaine, Moore, Rodin and others, because of his facility with a cocktail shaker." That would be Mike Mery, Jimmie's predecessor at the Dingo.

But Harrow and Mike had some help in putting the Dingo on the map, mainly from Florence "Flossie" Martin. Jimmie claimed that she "knew every Englishman and American in Montparnasse, brought all her friends and within a few days the place was so crowded that there was rarely a table free at drinking hours." So now they needed an assistant barman. Jimmie had been working at the Hole in the Wall* on the Right Bank, and got a tip from an "agent for Bacardi

---

* See "Six Characters in Search of an Author—with a Gun!" (page 74).

rum" about the Dingo's transformation, and was hired. After Jimmie had been there awhile, Mike got into bad habits with both drink and embezzlement, and had to go. Jimmie was promoted to head barman, and the rest is cocktail history. For his part, Harrow could never get used to the Anglo-American crowd and sold the Dingo to Louis Wilson and his wife, Jopi, in the autumn of 1924.

☛ **TASTING NOTE:** Shaking this drink vigorously gives it a nice, frothy head, which also helps to hide the somewhat murky brown color. The drink has a nice balance of sour, bitter, and sweet with bright citrus notes and, oddly enough, hints of Coca-Cola. If you don't have Dubonnet, a good sweet vermouth works well, such as Dolin Rouge. Or try Byrrh, which is more reflective of quinquina of that era.

FLORENCE "FLOSSIE" MARTIN

So who was this Flossie? She was a dancer with the famous Ziegfeld Follies, and was described as "a New York chorus girl who had been sent to Paris for voice training. 'But,' said Jimmie Charters, 'she did a little studying and finally stopped entirely.'" I think it's safe to say she kind of let herself go when she came to Paris. She became, along with Kiki,* one of the Queens of Montparnasse, famous for her drinking, her bawdy songs, and her charismatic personality.

Robert McAlmon referred to her as "a dashing bit of colour, of the Rubens type. Her orange hair was piled neatly about her clear, baby-smooth skin. It was easy to believe that the Flossie of a few years back, when some pounds lighter, had been one of the more dazzling of Ziegfeld's show girls." Ernest Hemingway described her as "a splendid sort of two-hundred-pound meteoric glad girl," and

* See Kiki Cocktail (page 124).

"the only really gay person during the time I frequented the Quarter." A deleted portion of *The Sun Also Rises* likely refers to her: "The Quarter characters are not happy except for the girl who can always be depended upon to shout obscenities and whose complexion, appetite and ability to get blind drunk night after night and be as cheerful as a young calf remains the same although she is getting to weigh well over two hundred pounds makes her the heroine of the Quarter."

Florence "Flossie" Martin with a friend on rue Delambre, near the Dingo. PHOTOGRAPH COURTESY OF THE KAY BOYLE PAPERS COLLECTION, SPECIAL COLLECTIONS RESEARCH CENTER, MORRIS LIBRARY, UNIVERSITY OF SOUTHERN ILLINOIS.

And it wasn't just the Dingo that benefitted from Flossie's influence. Indeed, "Joe Zelli, the Montmartre night-club king, gave Flossie a so-called 'job,' paying her simply to be in his club every night since her mere presence and exuberant gaiety would attract a crowd." It worked; "Zelli did the biggest business of his career during the six months Flossie stayed at his club!"

Flossie "was a friend of all the world, and around her was always to be found a group of English, Americans, and French, all infected by her somewhat loud but happy laughter." Tourists passing through, sailors on liberty, anyone who met her might fall under her spell and send her postcards from afar after they'd moved on. In some instances, "postcards addressed simply, 'Miss Flossie Martin, Somewhere near the Dingo, France,' reached her."

One Bastille Day, McAlmon recalled that "it was impossible not to hear Florence Martin as soon as I entered the Quarter. She was at the Dôme bar, electing herself Dowager of the Dôme, Queen of Montmartre and Montparnasse . . . Queen Bee of drinkers." Sometimes, though, her act could wear a little thin. McAlmon recalled an epic, all-night spree. At ten the next morning, he found himself at the outdoor terrace of the Dôme with Hilaire Hiler, Thelma Wood, and a few others. Upon hearing that "Flossie Martin was asleep at one of the tables inside," McAlmon "became wise and grabbed a taxi, knowing that Flossie would waken and descend upon us all, insisting upon drink and more drink." And for what it's worth, James Joyce was decidedly not a fan of Flossie; "he had difficulty in believing that such a person really existed."

The title of Jimmie's memoir, *This Must Be the Place*, comes from a classic Flossie tale. As more and more tourists came to Paris, the expats saw them as pests, "mere curiosity seekers who came to look at 'the wild artists in their den." Further, they "went completely beserk the minute they hit Montparnasse." One evening, Jimmie was walking from the Dôme to the Dingo, with Flossie a few paces ahead, same destination in mind. Just then, "a handsome Rolls-Royce drove up to the curb and from it stepped two lavishly-dressed ladies." They were also Dingo-bound, but they hesitated, peering into the windows, unsure. Flossie breezed past them and, to show her contempt for the tourists, "she tossed a single phrase over her shoulder: 'You bitch!' Whereupon wthe lady so addressed nudged her companion anxiously. 'Come on, Helen,' she said. 'This must be the place!'"

RHUM SAINT-JAMES COCKTAIL

2–3 ounces Rhum Saint-James
¹/₃ ounce simple syrup
½ ounce orange curaçao
½ ounce anisette
6 drops Angostura aromatic bitters
Lemon peel, for zest and to garnish

Stir well with ice, then strain into a chilled highball glass half filled with ice, zest a lemon peel atop the drink and either discard or drop the peel into the drink as garnish. Serve with two straws (see illustration, page 167).

Recipe from 156 Recettes de Boissons Américaines *(1920)*.

RHUM SAINT-JAMES IS A BRAND FROM MARTINIQUE. AS is the case with many French Caribbean rums, it is a rhum agricole. See, there are basically two kinds of rum. "Industrial rum," made from molasses, is the most common. Meanwhile, rhum agricole is made directly from the sugar-cane juice. It often has a funkier scent and flavor, and that's not a bad thing. Cachaça, the cane spirit of Brazil, is also made from the juice, but we're not supposed to call it rum. But that's a whole other story.

This cocktail goes back to at least the 1880s. Many people assume that rum (and rum drinks) were not popular in 1920s Paris. Au contraire, they were (and still are). It is easier to understand when you

Cover of the 1932 edition of 156 Recettes de Boissons Américaines. IMAGE COURTESY OF COLLECTIF 1806.

consider that France isn't just *continental* France; it's made up of juris-dictional divisions known as "departments." Several of them are located overseas, notably the Society Islands (Tahiti, Bora Bora, et al.), Guadeloupe, Corse (Corsica), and, of course, Martinique.

During the 1920s, most Parisians gravitated toward beer, wine, apéritifs, and other locally produced products, while Anglo-American expats tended toward spirits, e.g., whiskey and gin. Part of this was cultural, part of it was a matter of economics. To every general rule there are exceptions, and in this case it's rum and brandy (including Cognac, Armagnac, Calvados, and other regional brandies). As was noted in Robert Forrest Wilson's 1930 book *Paris on Parade*:

Of the spirits, it should be noted that they are extremely expensive in France, except for brandy, a Dômestic French product, and rum, which is imported from the French colony, Martinique. Scotch whisky sells for prices that, to an American, are high and to a Frenchman prohibitive.

As perhaps a harbinger of his eventual years in true rum country (he moved to Key West in 1931 and Cuba in 1939), Ernest Hemingway cut his rhum teeth during his Paris years. As we covered in the chapter on Grog *Americain* (page 95), he told Sherwood Anderson of the Hot Rum Punch he and his wife enjoyed at the Dôme Café, noting that "the rhum enters into us like the Holy Spirit." Three days later he bragged to his friend Howell Jenkins that their apartment "looks like a fine Grog shop—Rhum, Asti Spumante and Cinzano Vermouth fill one shelf. I brew a rum punch that'd gaol you. Living is very cheap. . . . I get rum for 14 francs a bottle. Vive la France." Hemingway later wrote to Jenkins that "I'm drinking Rum St. James now with rare success. It is the genuwind [*sic*] 7-year old rum as smooth as a kitten's chin."

Rhum Saint-James is also found in Hemingway's memoir, *A Moveable Feast*, where he reminisced about writing on a cold Paris day. "I ordered a rum St. James [*sic*]. This tasted wonderful on the cold day and I kept on writing, feeling very well and feeling the good Martinique rum warm me all through my body and my spirit."

☞ **TASTING NOTE:** If you don't have Rhum Saint-James, try another rhum agricole, such as Depaz or Clément, both of which make for a delicious cocktail. Plantation Rum's bottlings from Guadeloupe are also superb, and Ferrand Dry Curaçao is a fine choice here.

PARIS, THE CITY OF SKYLIGHTS?

Throughout his life, Ernest Hemingway was known for being somewhat accident-prone. While many of his injuries were due to his adventurous lifestyle (plane crashes on African safari, fishing or hunting mishaps, et cetera), others were just bad luck. For example, one night in 1928, Ernest and his new bride Pauline had dinner with Archibald and Ada MacLeish. They returned to their apartment on rue Ferou, and at 2:00 a.m. Ernest used the bathroom. Perhaps it was because it was the middle of the night, perhaps it was that Hem had had a few; in any event, he tugged and tugged on the flush-toilet chain until . . . he learned the hard way that it wasn't the toilet chain. It was intended to open the skylight in the ceiling of the bathroom. Apparently, the skylight's wood frame had rotted, and the entire thing, metal casement and all, came crashing down on Hemingway's head. Blood was everywhere.

As he wrote to his editor Max Perkins, "We stopped the hemmorage ⟨sic⟩ with 30 thicknesses of toilet paper (a magnificent absorbent which I've now used twice for that purpose in pretty much emergencies), and a tourniquet of kitchen towel and a stick of kindling wood." They raced to the American Hospital in Neuilly, where (Hemingway later claimed) an American doctor named Carl Weiss closed the wound with nine stitches. If that name rings a bell, there was a Dr. Carl Weiss who lived in Paris in the 1920s, and he later moved to Baton Rouge, Louisiana. In September 1935, Weiss assassinated Senator Huey Long, the Kingfish of Louisiana. That said, another source maintains that Hemingway's noggin was sewn up by a Dr. Sumner Waldron Jackson of Maine. As often is the case, a good Hemingway yarn often gets fouled up by those pesky facts.

When Hemingway's friend Ezra Pound learned of the mishap, he wrote, in true Ezra fashion, "how the hellsufferin tomcats did you git drunk enough to fall upwards through the blithering skylight?" When it came to colorful expression such as this, there was no one better than Ezra.

In front of Shakespeare and Company bookstore, spring of 1928. Left to right are Myrsine and Hélène Moschos, Sylvia Beach, and a heavily bandaged Ernest Hemingway. PHOTOGRAPH COURTESY OF THE SYLVIA BEACH PAPERS, MANUSCRIPTS DIVISION, DEPARTMENT OF RARE BOOKS AND SPECIAL COLLECTIONS, PRINCETON UNIVERSITY LIBRARY, PRINCETON, NEW JERSEY.

ROSE COCKTAIL

Barflies and Cocktails (1927) version, and attributed to Johnny Mitta at the Hôtel Chatham bar

2 ounces dry vermouth

½ ounce kirschwasser

½ ounce red currant syrup

Maraschino cherry, for garnish

Stir well with ice, then strain into a chilled cocktail glass, garnish with a maraschino cherry.

◆——◇——◆

The Artistry of Mixing Drinks (1936) version, and also attributed to Mitta

2 ounces dry vermouth

1 ounce kirschwasser

1 teaspoon raspberry syrup

Maraschino cherry, for garnish

Stir well with ice, then strain into a chilled cocktail glass, garnish with a maraschino cherry.

◆——◇——◆

370 Recettes de Cocktails (1928) version

¾ ounce London dry gin

¾ ounce Noilly Prat dry vermouth

¾ ounce kirschwasser

2 dashes crème de cassis

1 dash strawberry syrup

Maraschino cherry, for garnish

Stir well with ice, then strain into a chilled cocktail glass, garnish with a maraschino cherry.

Cocktails de Paris (1929) version

1½ ounces dry vermouth
¾ ounce kirschwasser
³/₈ ounce Cherry Heering
³/₈ ounce red currant syrup
Maraschino cherry, for garnish

Stir well with ice, then strain into a chilled cocktail glass, garnish with a maraschino cherry.

370 Recettes de Cocktails (1928), additional version created by the book's author, Jean Lupoiu

½ ounce London dry gin
½ ounce sweet vermouth
½ ounce dry vermouth
½ ounce kirschwasser
2 dashes Cherry Heering
2 dashes red currant syrup
1 dash crème de noyaux
1 dash maraschino liqueur

Stir well with ice, then strain into a chilled cocktail glass, garnish with a maraschino cherry.

NSPIRED BY THE IMMORTAL GERTRUDE STEIN QUOTE "A rose is a rose is a rose," I'm offering you not one, not three, but five variations on the mighty-like-a-rose Rose Cocktail. And be assured, they all smell (and taste) as sweet. Why so many? As the great Robert Vermeire noted in his classic 1938 cocktail book, *l'Art du Cocktail*: "*Ce cocktail a une spécialité tout à fait exceptionnelle, parce qu'il n'est jamais fait de la même façon nulle part.*" Which translates to: "This cocktail is a specialty all done exceptionally, because it is never done the same way anywhere." No truer words were ever spoken.

While most accounts attribute the original drink's authorship to Johnny Mitta at the Hôtel Chatham bar in Paris, a few sources disagree. Indeed, in the 1928 book *370 Recettes de Cocktails Par Jean Lupoiu*, the drink is credited to someone named Santos at the Chatham. Meanwhile, the 1929 book *Cocktails de Paris*, written by Georges Gabriel Thenon, claimed Albert at the Chatham did the deed. Perhaps there was a chap named Albert Santos, who knows? But for what it's worth, Robert Vermeire flat out said that "*Le créateur incontestable est Johnie, du Chatham Bar in Paris.*" And that's good enough *pour moi*.

Regardless of its parentage, it's a fine drink and was quite popular in 1920s Paris. *How to Wine and Dine in Paris* (1930) noted that "the two Parisian specialties in cocktails are the Rose and the Champagne Cocktail," and referred to the Rose as "easily the favorite with French women."

Vintage ad from the Hôtel Chatham, the likely birthplace of the Rose.
FROM THE AUTHOR'S
COLLECTION.

☞ **TASTING NOTE:** As for the recipes found in this chapter, try them all and see which ones you fancy. I'm partial to two of them. The *Barflies and Cocktails* version is very simple, just vermouth, kirsch, and crème de cassis. Jean Lupoiu's is a bit more complicated; the crème de noyaux (such as Tempus Fugit or Noyau de Poissy) adds a nutty nuance to the drink, and the gin, some extra backbone. For the maraschino liqueur, go with either Luxardo or Leopold Bros.

KIRSCHWASSER

The Rose is a great introduction to kirschwasser, the classic cherry brandy popular in France and the Alpine regions, and a favorite drink of Ernest Hemingway and John Dos Passos. During a 1923 visit to Schruns, Austria, the locals called the bearded Hemingway "the Black Kirsch-drinking Christ." In a letter to his friend Bill Smith, he noted that "they got a Kirch ⟨*sic*⟩ down here that you cant taste the alc in at all. No burn to it. But grand wallop. We punished 18 of them yest"

Hemingway rented a fourth-floor room in Paris as a writing studio, "and it was warm and pleasant to work." He would eat "mandarins and roasted chestnuts" while he worked, and kept "a bottle of kirsch that we had brought back from the mountains and I took a drink of kirsch when I would get towards the end of a story or towards the end of the day's work."

Dos Passos accompanied Ernest and Hadley, along with Sara and Gerald Murphy, on a 1926 trip to Schruns. He fondly recalled that "the Kirsch was so plentiful they gave it to us to rub off with when we came in from skiing."

ROSE GERANIUM MARTINI A'LA CARESSE CROSBY

> **2 ounces London dry gin**
> **1 ounce dry vermouth**
> **½ ounce rose geranium syrup or liqueur**
>
> ---
>
> Stir all ingredients well with ice, then strain into a chilled cocktail glass.
>
> *Recipe from* Cocktails of the Paris Ritz by Colin Peter Field *(2003).*

THIS IS ANOTHER FROM THE CANON OF THAT SWINGIN' couple Harry and Caresse Crosby.* While Harry's diary contained a number of hedonistic moments, Caresse's had a few of her own. They often held decadent soirées at their opulent rue de Lille town house. Said Caresse:

> When we wanted to be entertained we received in bed. . . . We always drank champagne and we almost always began with caviar. Our guests were invited to take baths if they wanted to, for we had a sunken marble tub and a black and white tile bathroom that boasted a white bearskin rug and an open fireplace, as well as a cushioned chaise lounge [*sic*] covered in rose red toweling. We liked to experi-

---

* See the Alaska Cocktail (page 8), the Quat'z'Arts "Tremendous Punch" (page 99), and the Sherry Cobbler (page 183).

ment with bath oils and bath salts. . . . Chez nous martinis and rose geranium mingled in libation. Some evenings were rather Pompeiian. The bath could hold four.

When I first encountered this diary entry, I wasn't sure what Caresse meant about those drinks. "Chez nous martinis and rose geranium mingled in libation"—what on earth does that mean? It took a bit of thinking, then, okay, so they made homemade Martinis, and they must have "experimented" with some of their bath oils, and were particularly pleased with the addition of rose geranium oil to their Martini.

Rose geranium oil is popular in the field of aromatherapy, and some brands are edible. While I've not yet tried any of these products, I have found a very nice rose geranium liqueur from BroVo Spirits, out of Portland, Oregon.

As an aside, Harry and Caresse weren't the only colorful characters of 1920s Paris experimenting with the classic Martini. Indeed, poet, occultist, and "diabolist" Aleister Crowley invented his own version, which he'd serve to friends (including artist and writer Nina Hamnett) at his flat on rue Vavin in Montparnasse. He called it the Kubla Khan No. 2, and it was your basic gin and vermouth Martini, with the addition of laudanum, a potent opium-based narcotic. Seems fitting for a sun-worshipper (Crosby) and a devil-worshipper (Crowley) to have similarly exotic notions about mixology, and perhaps we should leave it at that.

☞ **TASTING NOTE:** This is a delicious change of pace from the regular Dry Martini. Like Harry and Caresse, you can experiment with the amount of the rose geranium liqueur. Adding just a dash adds a very nice floral nose to the drink. Rose flower water also works well.

R⊘YAL HIGHBALL

> **1 ounce Cognac**
> **4 ripe strawberries, plus an extra, for garnish**
> **4 ounces Champagne**
>
> ---
>
> Muddle the strawberries with the Cognac in the bottom of a mixing tin. Transfer to a tall highball glass filled with ice. Slowly add the Champagne. Stir well or swizzle to dredge up the fruit, and garnish with a whole strawberry.

ALTHOUGH THE HOTEL RITZ PARIS OPENED ITS DOORS on the Place Vendôme back in 1898, its celebrated bar did not come to be for over two decades. In the words of my friend Colin Field, head bartender at the Ritz's legendary Bar Hemingway:

> The story . . . begins in 1921, when it was decided to create a room for alcoholic refreshment in the Cambon Wing. . . . The Head Bartender was to be Frank Meier, and he would receive the world's elite. Sir Winston Churchill, President Theodore Roosevelt, Noël Coward, F. Scott Fitzgerald and Cole Porter, to name but a few. It was at this time, incidentally, that Frank Meier invented the Royal Highball (a marvelously refreshing drink made with cognac, strawberries and Champagne) for the King of Spain.

And his would be a magnificent reign of more than twenty-five years.

I'm speaking of Frank Meier, of course, not King Alfonso XIII (who was no great shakes as a king). Truly, Frank was one of the kings of the cocktail scene of Paris, or even of the world. In *The Paris That's Not in the Guidebooks*, Basil Woon referred to Frank as "possibly the best-known drink shaker in the world, not excluding the individual who does it at the Savoy in London." It's interesting to note that both Frank and the Savoy's Harry Craddock worked at Manhattan's famed Hoffman House prior to crossing the Pond.

Woon further noted that "Frank is the most feared man in Parisian society" because of the secrets he holds. *Paris with the Lid Lifted* agreed: "Frank, manager of this astounding shrine . . . can socially make or break a visitor, depending upon the degree of the cordiality of his greeting. To be addressed by Frank, by name, is no mean compliment. And he is the intimate of the scions of great families of America. Millionaires make Frank their confidant and give him tips on the stock market. He knows the business connections, the social connections of all."

Frank, author of the immortal *The Artistry of Mixing Drinks* (1936), ran the Ritz Bar through World War II (during which he was a hero of the French Resistance, though those stories are from another decade, and belong in another book). He summed up a key part of his philosophy as follows:

> To know how to drink is as essential as to know how to swim, and one should be at home in both these closely related elements. Each man reacts differently to alcohol; he should know before the time when, according to custom, he indulges in his first collegiate "binge," whether liquor affects his head, his legs or his morals; whether he sings, fights, weeps, climbs lamp posts or behaves with excessive affection toward the opposite sex; whether, in short, it makes him a jovial companion or a social pest. A knowledge of these weaknesses will help to overcome them. . . . "In vino veritas," so often quoted, does not mean that a man will tell the truth when in drink, but will reveal the hidden side of his character.

And I will drink to that.

One final note, Frank wasn't the only one in Paris doing some creative things with Champagne and strawberries. Aleister Crowley,

Frank Meier, head bartender,
Paris Ritz Bar, 1921–1947.
PHOTOGRAPH COURTESY OF
JEAN-FRÉDÉRIC SCHALL AND THE
ROGER SCHALL COLLECTION.

quite known for his mixological (and black magic) chops himself, created a drink he called the Crowley Cup No. 3, which he described thusly: "Take a large jug, the larger the better; half fill with selected strawberries; cover the fruit with Grand Marnier Cordon Rouge; ice carefully; fill up with iced champagne, the best obtainable. Stir the mixture; drink it; order more; and repeat." Nothing evil about this drink; in fact, it's wicked good!

☛ **TASTING NOTE:** This is another excellent introduction to the wonders of Cognac, as the strawberries (the riper, the better) and bubbly enliven and soften the complexity of the spirit. This is an excellent brunch drink.

SCOFF-LAW COCKTAIL

1 ounce rye whiskey
1 ounce dry vermouth
½ ounce fresh lemon juice
½ ounce grenadine
1 dash orange bitters
Cherry or lemon peel, for garnish

Stir or shake well with ice, then strain into a chilled cocktail glass. Garnish with a maraschino cherry or lemon peel.

Recipe from Barflies and Cocktails *(1927).*

THE SCOFF-LAW COCKTAIL IS ONE OF (AT LEAST) FOUR drinks on the menu at Harry's New York Bar that poked fun at Prohibition.* There was a gent named Delcevere King, of Quincy, Massachusetts, a staunch supporter of the Volstead Act. He wanted to coin a new word for "a drinker of liquor made or obtained illegally— a lawless drinker."

So King staged a contest to develop such a term, offering a whopping $200 in prize money. He recruited as fellow judges the Reverend E. Talmadge Root (the secretary of the Massachusetts Federation of Churches) and A. J. Davis (regional superintendent of the Anti-Saloon League of America). Yep, the original rat pack. This

---

* See also the Three Mile Limit (page 201), the Twelve-Mile Cocktail (page 208), and the Volstead Cocktail (page 226).

august panel sifted through no less than twenty-five thousand entries "from forty-eight states and several foreign countries." As criteria, King noted that the "epithet should be preferably one or two syllables" and "it should preferably begin with 's,'" since "'S' words have a sting." Further, the new word had to "stab awake the conscience of the lawless drinker."

On January 16, 1924, newspapers around this great land carried the news that the term "scoff-law," offered by two people (Irving Shaw of Shawsheen, Massachusetts, and Miss Kate L. Battler of Boston—presumably they split the prize), was the winner.

Ten days later, "Jock, the genial bartender of Harry's New York Bar, . . . invented the Scofflaw Cocktail." The *Chicago Tribune* summed it up with a bit of cheek, noting that "hardly has Boston added to the Gaeity of Nations by adding to *Webster's Dictionary* the opprobrious term of 'scoff-law,' . . . when Paris comes back with a 'wet answer.'" The story further noted that the drink was already "exceedingly popular among American prohibition dodgers." Harry's actively promoted their Prohibition-poking potables; behind the bar hung signs reading: TRY OUR SCOFFLAW COCKTAIL and A DRINK WITH A KICK—TRY THE THREE MILE LIMIT.

☞ **TASTING NOTE:** Prohibition-era drinks often get a bad rap, but the Scoff-law is one of the good ones. Just be sure to use a true (pomegranate) grenadine, and not one with fructose corn syrup and red food coloring. You deserve better.

AIN'T MISBEHAVIN', MUCH . . .

While we're on the topic of scoffin' at the law, I'll tell you a few tales of expats getting into a little trouble with the police.

One evening, John Dos Passos, poet E. E. Cummings, and Gilbert Seldes had dinner at Café de la Paix. Then, "full of wine and François Villon and Cummings' imagery," they headed off to a little boîte or club that Cummings had suggested. On their way there, Cummings felt nature's call and chose "a particularly dark little alley . . . for the purpose of taking a leak. Immediately he was seized by a pair of *agents de police* . . . who appeared from nowhere. '*Un pisseur*,' they cried, and marched him off to the police station." Dos Passos followed, explaining in "noisy French" that Cummings was "America's greatest poet" and also that all three of them had served in World War I, all the while mixing in plenty of "*viva la France* and *vive l'Amérique*" for good measure. Nevertheless, Cummings was booked and given a trial date the next day. Fortunately, after Seldes called in a few favors, the charges were dropped. Cummings later concluded, "If you're going to get drunk it's safer to wear a dress suit." Perhaps he would have agreed with H. L. Mencken's flippant remark about the city's public urinals: "The cafés of Paris dangerously outnumber the *pissoirs*."

Another memorable occasion was what Ernest Hemingway called Jimmie Charters's "greatest socking exploit in Montparnasse." It happened at the place where so many scenes seemed to occur—at the Sélect. Djuna Barnes, Thelma Wood, and a friend were having a few drinks, and Robert McAlmon and Ian Meyers were seated nearby. Jimmie had the night off and joined them for a round. All of a sudden, "then came swinging into the bar an internationally known American newspaperman, . . . roaring drunk. Focusing on Djuna, he lunged toward her and . . . began pawing and mauling her in a manner no gentleman would use." It might be helpful to note that Djuna and Thelma were lovers. Jimmie managed to remove him from

Djuna, got him to another table, and bought him a drink, but he refused to leave.

Next thing you know, Djuna came over and gave him "a piece of her mind." The man jumped up and knocked her to the ground with "a well-placed blow to the chin," and then sent McAlmon, Meyers, and the other two girls "sprawled to the sidewalk." Eventually Jimmie, a former boxer, got into the melee and knocked the man down three times. "The next day," Jimmie recalled, "he did not remember who had hit him . . ." Sadly, we don't know who this "internationally known American newspaperman" was; Jimmie didn't identify him, as "it might hurt him in business" to do so. You've got to love a bartender with discretion.

Another story also concerns McAlmon and Charters. It seems they were both at Bricktop's in Montmartre. McAlmon and Ada "Bricktop" Smith were old friends, and when the pair arrived, she jokingly said to him, "Give me a kiss." Always the kidder, McAlmon playfully shook his fist at her and said, "I will give you a punch instead!" One of the staff misunderstood and was quickly all over McAlmon like a cheap suit, but "Bob was quicker and sent him sprawling. Soon the whole place was in turmoil." Charters later recalled, "Bob and I spent the night in jail, but we thought it was well worth it."

SHERRY COBBLER

2 ounces Sherry
1 ounce brandy
1 ounce orange curaçao
1 teaspoon sugar
Orange slices, for garnish
1 ounce Port wine

Fill a shaker two-thirds full with crushed ice. Add all ingredients but the Port, then shake vigorously. Transfer contents to a tall glass or wineglass. Garnish with two orange slices, over which you'll gently pour the Port. Serve with two straws.

Recipe from 156 Recettes de Boissons Américaines *(1920).*

THE SHERRY COBBLER IS AN AMERICAN CLASSIC, FROM well before the Civil War, and perhaps the first drink to be enjoyed with a straw. France's proximity to Sherry (from Spain) made this a natural in Paris. But, as is the case with the Jack Rose, they made it a bit differently there. In the 1921 book *Paris Days and London Nights*, you'll find the passage, "We drank what the Parisians call *un sherry gobbleur*. It wasn't at all according to our idea of what a sherry cobbler should be but it was cool and refreshing." In Paris, they often added Cognac, maraschino, curaçao, cassis, even cherry brandy, not to mention that float of Port.

While typically a white wine drinker, James Joyce enjoyed Sherry Cobblers with Ernest Hemingway one evening at Deux Magots on the boulevard Saint-Germain. The drink was a staple at the historic Restaurant Ledoyen, located in a beautiful park just off the Champs-Élysées. Ledoyen was especially popular in summer, when "tables are set in the open space before the door, and one may dine delightfully beneath the trees." Back in the summer of 1929, you might have seen Harry Crosby enjoying a few.

His diary describes July 18 in typical unabashed, stream-of-consciousness fashion, noting that he and Caresse (C) "dined at Ledoyen one sherry cobbler two sherry cobblers three sherry cobblers and so home and to bed C looking lovely in her yellow dress and out of her yellow dress and loveliest with her Chanel imitation-ice necklace." The next day Harry and Caresse were back at Ledoyen for supper, and "after innumerable sherry cobblers" they stopped at the post office to send a cable home: "Please sell ten thousand dollars worth of stock—we have decided to lead a mad and extravagant life." One wonders, how might these two swingers have characterized their life in Paris prior to that?

Sherry Cobblers also played a minor role in the drama surrounding poet Hart Crane's arrest and imprisonment that same summer. Harry was serving as something of a mentor to Crane, as he struggled to complete his epic poem, *The Bridge*, even offering him lodging. In Crosby's diary entry of June 28, he groused, "Hart C. back from Marseille where he slept with his thirty sailors and he began again to drink Cutty Sark (the last bottle in the house)." One night shortly thereafter, like a few others had also done (notably Robert McAlmon), Crane got into a row with the co-owner of Le Sélect, known as "Madame Sélect." The dispute was "apparently because of his refusal to pay for the drinks he had. This at least was her interpretation of Hart's wild French and his antic gestures." After much smashing of furniture, the cops arrived, Hart was arrested, and thrown into La Santé Prison.

Although Harry paid Hart's bail, "they wouldn't let him out right away," so Crosby naturally dashed off to Ledoyen with a friend "to eat and to drink sherry cobblers in the sun. We got tight and we went off to see Eugene O'Neill and then I went to the bank." If that wasn't enough, on his way back to La Santé, Crosby "saw a pretty girl," chatted her up, then spirited her off to the Ritz for, you guessed it, a Sherry Cobbler. Her name was Sheelah, if you're keeping track. When they still wouldn't release Crane, Harry and friends retired to a nearby bar, to drink beer and play checkers. After nearly a week in prison, Crane was finally released, "unshaved hungry wild." As insult to injury, Crosby wrote, "The dirty skunks in the Santé wouldn't give him any paper to write poems on. The bastards."

☛ **TASTING NOTE:** Use a good dry Sherry as the Port and curaçao can make it too sweet. This is a gorgeous drink, and mellows in the glass as the ice melts. This one can convert a non-Sherry fan, including yours truly.

SIDECAR

1½ ounces Cognac or brandy
¾ ounce Cointreau
¾ ounce fresh lemon juice

Shake well with ice, then strain into a chilled cocktail glass.

Recipe from The Artistry of Mixing Drinks *(1936).*

THE CREATOR OF THE IMMORTAL SIDECAR ("SIDE-CAR," at Harry's, and "Side Car," at the Ritz) remains an unsolved cocktail mystery. In his 1948 classic, *The Fine Art of Mixing Drinks*, David Embury claimed that "it was invented by a friend of mine at a bar in Paris during World War I after the motorcycle sidecar in which the good captain customarily was driven to and from the little bistro where the drink was born and christened." That said, in both Harry MacElhone's *ABC of Mixing Cocktails* (1923) and Robert Vermeire's *Cocktails: How to Mix Them* (1922), credit is given to "MacGarry, the popular Bartender at Buck's Club, London." But in Lucius Beebe's 1946 gem, *The Stork Club Bar Book*, he emphatically stated that "so far as fallible human memory can determine," Frank Meier of the Paris Ritz Bar invented it, made with "Ritz's own bottling of a vintage 1865 Cognac," which "set one back . . . the equivalent of five American dollars."

Irrespective of its parentage, the Sidecar was quite popular in 1920s Paris. Its ascendance was noted in the 1930 guide *How To Wine and Dine in Paris*: "By and large, the Martini is the standard cocktail

Milan, summer of 1918, an eighteen-year-old International Red Cross ambulance driver named Ernest Hemingway goes for a spin in a motorcycle sidecar. PHOTOGRAPH COURTESY OF THE ERNEST HEMINGWAY COLLECTION. JOHN F. KENNEDY PRESIDENTIAL LIBRARY AND MUSEUM, BOSTON.

in Paris, just as it is in America, though there is a rising market in Sidecars."

American expat Gerald Murphy, creator of the Bailey (page 26) and Juice of a Few Flowers (page 120), made his own variation on the Sidecar, which he called the Villa America Special. His daughter Honoria described the drink as "brandy, a liqueur, and lemon juice, which he poured from a silver shaker into long-stemmed glasses, the rims of which had been rubbed with lemon and dipped in coarse sugar." While we don't know Gerald's choice of liqueur, it shows how versatile the drink's format is, as you can swap out a different liqueur and give the drink its own personality.

Novelist Carl Van Vechten featured the Sidecar throughout his novel *Parties: Scenes from Contemporary New York Life*. It's the tale of a dissolute young American named David who, among other escapades, meets a young woman, Mrs. Alonzo W. Syreno, on a transatlantic crossing.

She's going to Paris to divorce her much-older millionaire husband, and during a binge of double Sidecars, David figures why not join her? He later finds himself embracing "the warmth and snugness of the Castiglione Bar," where Otto the bartender makes "a succession of sidecars." Afterward, while David took a cab to Larue's, "a pleasant glow warmed his veins, a sensation that is within the reach of anyone who can afford to drink the proper number of sidecars." David reasoned, "There was something about the atmosphere of Paris that gave an extra tang to a sidecar, or any other drink whatever." I cannot disagree with him.

☞ **TASTING NOTE:** The Sidecar is an excellent introduction to the flavors of Cognac, a "gateway drink," so to speak. The key is to use fresh lemon juice and a good quality orange liqueur; avoid those bottom-shelf triple secs! Further, you might take a lesson from Murphy and try different liqueurs to add some variety. Domaine de Canton gives the drink a spicy ginger flavor, or try Suze or Salers to add a little gentian-based bitterness.

THE LADY'S SIDE OF THE RITZ BAR

As noted earlier, novelist Carl Van Vechten has his character, the Sidecar-swigging Mrs. Syreno, heading to Paris for her divorce. Van Vechten was tapping into a cultural phenomenon of the day, as Paris had become a magnet for such women. "The quickie divorce was all the rage, and Paris was its center: the divorce mill of Europe."

Many recently divorced women spent their afternoons at the so-called "Ladies Bar" of the Paris Ritz. See, there wasn't just one Ritz Bar. Then, as now, when you enter the hotel from the rue Cambon, there's a bar on your left and one on your right. Today, the main bar is on the left, while the famed Bar Hemingway is on the right. But back in the 1920s, the bar on the right, nicknamed "the Black Hole of Calcutta" and "the steam room," was "where ladies might sip their cocktails. About six o'clock at night the place is filled to suffocation and has a delicate perfume faintly reminiscent of attar of roses in a bottle of old Bourbon." It was here that the divorcées gathered:

> Since it became fashionable to boast a Paris divorce, the Ritz ladies' room has been headquarters for the Alimony Sisterhood, who meet there and compare notes about past and future husbands, lawyers' fees, their dearest friends and the increasing popularity of pearl necklaces. . . . There are ladies making the Ritz bar a nightly ceremony who are at their fourth husband and won't admit to thirty years of age.

Apparently there was a Left Bank chapter to this exclusive "club"; Jimmie Charters recalled the "'alimony gang,' . . . women who came to Montparnasse after a divorce . . . Once there and established in an apartment, they looked around for company, only to find that the women in Montparnasse numbered two or three for every man. Yet there were some men available and the women came to the bars to find them."

Here's hoping the fictitious Mrs. Syreno found sorority and fellowship on the appropriate side of the Seine.

SPIRIT OF ST. LOUIS

3 ounces London dry gin
1 egg white
1 teaspoon grenadine
2 drops orange flower water

Shake very well, then strain into a chilled cocktail glass.

Recipe from ABC of Mixing Cocktails *(1934).*

THIS DRINK COMMEMORATES ONE OF THE MORE historic feats in the annals of aviation, Charles Lindbergh's solo crossing of the Atlantic Ocean. Although the Wright brothers' first flight was way back in 1903, by 1927, no one had crossed the Atlantic in an "aeroplane." A man named Raymond Orteig had offered a $25,000 prize for the first nonstop flight, and many suitors lined up for the award, and the glory. The people of France were caught up in the excitement as two decorated French aviators, Charles Nungesser and his partner, François Coli, threw their chapeau into the ring. On May 8, 1927, they took off from Paris's Le Bourget airport in their biplane, called *l'Oiseau Blanc*, the "White Bird." Its goal: Roosevelt Field, Long Island. All France held its collective breath.

L'Oiseau Blanc disappeared somewhere over the Atlantic.

Despite their profound sadness, the idea of the world's first transatlantic crossing gripped the French imagination, and all eyes now fixed on young Charles Lindbergh as he prepared his attempt. On Friday, May 20, the tiny single-engine airplane, the *Spirit of St. Louis*, took off from that same Roosevelt Field, with the destination that same Le Bourget. Excitement rose throughout Paris. Eric Hawkins, managing editor of the *Paris Herald Tribune*, recalled:

> We on the *Herald* and the French police had vastly underestimated the emotional impact on the French of a lone flyer in a single-motored plane setting out without ballyhoo for a destination that was unknown in every sense of the word. Lindbergh deeply touched the French imagination, and despite the earlier failure of their own airmen . . . they desperately wanted him to succeed.

Throughout the day, excitement (and crowds) grew. Sometime during the afternoon of May 21, the *Spirit of St. Louis* was sighted over Ireland. "Each new development sent fresh crowds of Parisians toward Le Bourget. . . . It was a fine clear night with a bright moon. A little after dark the word was flashed that Lindbergh had passed over Cherbourg, and from that moment on all of us knew he couldn't miss."

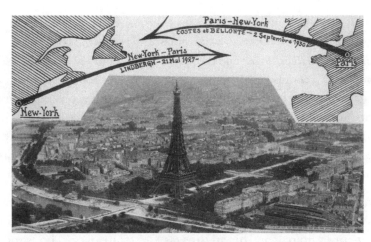

Souvenir postcard commemorating Lindbergh's successful solo flight from New York to Paris, as well as a subsequent flight in the opposite direction by Dieudonné Costes and Maurice Bellonte. FROM THE AUTHOR'S COLLECTION.

Cole Porter was among those awaiting Lindbergh's arrival. Harry and Caresse (C) Crosby and two friends also made the trek, having left for Le Bourget upon hearing Lindbergh was "two hundred miles off the coast of Ireland." They were "among the first to arrive and an hour later there is an enormous crowd." By ten o'clock "the crowd is impatient and there is a half-hearted attempt at a song and always the hiss of rockets and always the searching searchlights and I wish I had brought a coat and there is no gin left in my flask and C and I huddle together for warmth." As the suspense mounted, somehow an eerie calm came over the masses. Dead silence. Crosby thinks he hears "unmistakably the sound of an aeroplane . . . Is it Lindbergh?"

Meanwhile, up in the *Spirit of St. Louis*, the distant glow of Paris grew on the horizon, and "Lindbergh was drawn to it like a moth, and in its center stood the Eiffel Tower. He looped above it once, then headed" toward Le Bourget. During his approach, he was stunned to see the headlamps from thousands of cars as he was heading toward the air-field. It was Saturday night in Paris, just shy of ten thirty local time.

On the edge of the field, the Crosby party continued their vigil, gazing upward, listening . . .

> Then sharp swift in the gold glare of the searchlights a small white hawk of a plane swoops hawk-like down and across the field—*C'est lui Lindbergh, LINDBERGH!* and there is pandemonium wild animals let loose and a stampede ahead running people all round us running and the crowd behind stampeding like buffalo and a pushing and a shoving and . . . the extraordinary impression I had of hands thousands of hands weaving like maggots over the silver wings of the *Spirit of Saint-Louis* and it seems as if all the hands of the world are touching or trying to touch the new Christ.

Indeed, "as his wheels touched the ground, Lindbergh became the most famous man in the world." He'd been in the air more than thirty-three hours, but his night was far from over. Thousands of frenzied Parisians swarmed around the tiny *Spirit of St. Louis* and its intrepid pilot. The Lone Eagle had landed. Crosby's diary sums up the experience ("What an event!") with the simple phrase *"Ce n'est pas un homme, c'est un Oiseau!"* (He is not a man, he is a bird!)

Popular culture being what it is, cocktails were invented to honor the event, notably this chapter's subject, Harry MacElhone's Spirit of St. Louis cocktail. Meanwhile, across the Channel in jolly old London, the Savoy's Harry Craddock created a Charlie Lindbergh cocktail, made with Plymouth Gin, Kina Lillet, orange juice, and Pricota.

☞ **TASTING NOTE:** This is sort of a stripped-down version of the classic New Orleans drink the Ramos Gin Fizz, but without the cream, citrus, and seltzer. The recipe called for "one glass" of gin, meaning three ounces, but feel free to cut back on the gin and up the grenadine, to taste.

STINGER

> **2 ounces brandy**
> **1 ounce white crème de menthe**
>
> ---
>
> Shake well with ice, then strain into a chilled cocktail glass.
>
> *Recipe from* The Artistry of Mixing Drinks *(1936).*

LIKELY INVENTED IN THE FIRST FEW YEARS OF THE twentieth century, this drink was a pre-Prohibition favorite. Its debut was announced in a *New York Herald* story, described as an after-dinner cordial. "Here is something soothing and at the same time not devoid of tang. It makes visions to soothe the senses and warms the cocktails of the heart."

Writer and salon hostess Natalie Clifford Barney was apparently a Stinger fan. In her posthumously published novel *Women Lovers, or the Third Woman* (written in 1926, published in 2013), she placed a scene at one of her favorite Montparnasse watering holes, opening the chapter "Le Sélect" as follows:

> Downing his twentieth crème de menthe, McAc explains how he is superior to Shakespeare to anyone who would listen.
>
> Lady T.* sitting on her barstool, loses her haughtiness by drinking stingers."

---

* A footnote in this edition states that the Lady T. character "appears to refer to Una Troubridge, who frequented Le Sélect with Radclyffe Hall." And one wonders who McAc was—Robert McAlmon? Sinclair Lewis?

In his 1934 novel, *Tender Is the Night*, F. Scott Fitzgerald also saw fit to place the Stinger at another legendary Paris watering hole, the Ritz Bar. Here, Abe North (said to have been based on writer Ring Lardner*), "was still in the Ritz bar, where he had been since nine in the morning."

> By one o'clock the bar was jammed; amidst the consequent mixture of voices the staff of waiters functioned, pinning down their clients to the facts of drink and money. "That makes two stingers . . . and one more . . . two martinis and one . . . Mr. Schaeffer said he had this—you had the last . . . I can only do what you say . . . thanks vera-much."

Later, Abe relaxed, content with his drink; "he just sat, happy to live in the past. The drink made past happy things contemporary with the present, as if they were still going on, contemporary even with the future as if they were about to happen again."

It seems odd that ol' Abe had been in the Ritz Bar since nine a.m. Perhaps he'd not yet read Basil Woon's classic 1926 guide, *The Paris That's Not in the Guide Books*. Woon described the daily scene outside the hotel's rue Cambon entrance (nearest to the bar), where "a long line of thirsty citizens lined up, . . . waiting for twelve o'clock to strike so they may enter." Even though Woon noted that "the bar within has been open since ten o'clock," he explained that "no real American would ever dream of entering before twelve. It is one of the few things in Paris that really isn't done." Woon painted a vivid picture of the Ritz Bar:

> At 11:55 the big comfortable bar will be empty except for the waiters and maybe a lone pariah who has just got over and doesn't know the rules. But the waiters have a strained, expectant look, like runners awaiting the pistol's crack. At 11:59¼, the swing doors begin to revolve. At 12, eight cocktails are being drunk. At 12:02, the bar is filled.

---

* Fitzgerald often referred to Lardner as his "private drunkard; everybody had to have his private drunkard." John Dos Passos, *The Best Times* (New York: Signet, 1966), 168.

At 12:05, eleven friends know all about what you did at Kiley's or Zelli's last night. And so it goes.

It's also a bit odd that Fitzgerald's characters were ordering Stingers so early in the day. In *The Artistry of Mixing Drinks*, Ritz head bartender Frank Meier agreed with the *New York Herald* that the Stinger is "an after-dinner drink." But then, we're more than a little aware of the fact that F. Scott Fitzgerald sometimes broke the rules of polite society.

☛ **TASTING NOTE:** I repeat my previous advice to avoid those bottom-shelf liqueurs (such as crème de cassis and triple sec), as the choice of crème de menthe is make-or-break on this one; the results can range from ridiculous to sublime. Shun the cloying shade-of-green-not-found-in-nature offerings.

THE SOMETIMES NOT-SO-WELL-MANNERED FITZGERALDS

In the spring of 1925, fresh upon the release of *The Great Gatsby*, F. Scott and Zelda Fitzgerald moved to France. They "were looking to 'find a new rhythm' for their lives." Unfortunately, the days that followed were not particularly productive for F. Scott; in his diary, he called 1925 the summer of "1,000 parties and no work." But in a 1927 interview in the *New York World*, F. Scott donned his rose-colored glasses, noting that "the best of America drifts to Paris. The American in Paris is the best American. It is more fun for an intelligent person to live in an intelligent country. France has the only two things toward which we drift as we grow older—intelligence and good manners."

Really, F. Scott?

Let's just say that F. Scott and Zelda didn't always exhibit the best of manners. Perhaps they couldn't help it. As noted by Morrill Cody, "Scott and Zelda had little in common, yet the one passion they did share was very strong indeed. They were both 'excitement-eaters,' . . . a phrase that Zelda used in her book to describe herself." So, during the 1920s, the Fitzgeralds became "the most renowned 'excitement-eaters' of the western world." Their travels throughout Europe in the 1920s fed their appetites; Zelda would observe, "I hate a room without a suitcase in it—it seems so permanent." Gerald Murphy noted that they "did not seek ordinary pleasures. They wanted something unusual to happen, some act that they might not even understand," noting further that often "they worked together like a "pair of co-conspirators," and "intent on social sabotage." Zelda's friend Livye Hart said that "one of her

A couple of "excitement-eaters" if there ever were. F. Scott and Zelda Fitzgerald (with daughter, Scottie) pose for the family's 1925 Christmas photo, taken at their home on rue de Tilsitt, Paris.

main characteristics was her apparent delight in shocking people. And that was what she almost invariably did."

Writer Morley Callaghan remembered Zelda as having "the restless air, the little sway of a woman seeking some new exhilaration, a woman in Paris who knew the night should be just beginning." And sometimes it seemed to never end, with Zelda powerless to stop it: "Nobody knew whose party it was. It had been going on for weeks," she said. "When you felt you couldn't survive another night, you went home and slept and when you got back, a new set of people had consecrated themselves to keeping it alive."

Too often, Gerald and Sara Murphy bore the brunt of F. Scott and Zelda's mischief. One evening the four of them dined at La Colombe d'Or near Antibes, beloved by artists such as Pablo Picasso and Fernand Léger. Their table was "on the stone terrace overlooking the Loup valley, two hundred feet straight below . . ." At a nearby table sat the famous dancer Isadora Duncan. "Scott bounded over to introduce himself," and dropped to his knees. Duncan played along, and "ran her fingers through his hair and called him her centurion, which led to toasts with lukewarm champagne." While all eyes were on this absurd display, the quite-jealous Zelda "got to her feet and jumped over the parapet wall into the darkness." Off the cliff? "I was sure she was dead," Gerald recalled. "She had fallen onto a stone staircase that ran down from the terrace, and now she stood at the top, her knees and dress bloody, but otherwise unharmed." As they were leaving, the unfazed Zelda had the presence of mind to slip the glass automobile-shaped salt and pepper shakers into her purse.

And then there was the night that Sara and Gerald hosted a dinner party at Villa America for the Princess Chimay. During the evening, F. Scott "pursued a young man around the dance floor, asking him if he was a homosexual," and "during the dessert course, he threw a ripe fig down the back of the princess's décolletage. . . . Next, he began throwing Sara Murphy's prized Venetian glasses, full of liquor, over the garden wall, ruining her tomatoes." During another party where Ernest Hemingway was the guest of honor, F. Scott apparently felt that Sara was paying too much attention to

Hemingway. He began throwing ashtrays off the terrace, leered at women guests, then wrapped himself in a rug and crawled around the party, whining, "Sara's being mean to me." He then finished by insulting Gerald on how silly and pretentious the party was. That episode caused F. Scott to be banned from Villa America for three weeks, and prompted a stern letter from Sara, in which she said, "We *cannot . . . be bothered* with sophomoric situations—like last night . . . ," and she signed it, "Yr old & rather irritated friend, Sara."

It got so that their closest friends trembled with fear at the thought of their antics. In a letter to their mutual editor Maxwell Perkins, Hemingway begged: "Please don't under any circumstances give Scott our Paris home address—Last time he was in Paris he got us kicked out of one apt. and in trouble all the time (Insulted the landlord—pee-ed on the front porch—tried to break down the door at 3–4 and 5 a.m. etc.). . . . I am very fond of Scott but I'll beat him up before I'll let him come and get us ousted from this place. . . . When I heard he was going to Paris it gave me the horrors."

An entire book could be written about their antics, here are a few more instances:

According to legend, one evening in Paris, F. Scott and Zelda "entertained themselves by frivolously racing around the obelisk in the place de la Concorde in a stolen delivery-cart tricycle." But at least F. Scott got some literary juice out of the episode; he used it in his Paris short story, "Babylon Revisited."

The first time they lived in Paris, in May–June 1921, the dynamic duo likely didn't endear themselves among their neighbors at the Hôtel de Noailles (now the Hotel Saint James Albany). They lived on one of the upper floors, and wanted, no, *demanded* that they always have an elevator "on call" for them. How? Easy. Zelda blocked the elevator so it was always at their floor, at their ready disposal.

One evening in Monte Carlo, a doorman refused to allow F. Scott to enter the casino without his passport. F. Scott rebuked him with, "*Trés bien*, you son-of-a-bitch," and then passed out at his feet.

Another time, F. Scott and playwright Charles MacArthur were having a few in a bar, "disputing the possibility of sawing a man in half." To settle the matter, they somehow convinced a bartender to lie down between two chairs. MacArthur then produced a two-man saw (!). "The barman made such a commotion the police arrived." As he did with other such escapades, Fitzgerald worked it into his prose, this time it was *Tender Is the Night*, in which a very drunk Abe North tried to saw a waiter in half with a "musical saw."

Then there was that night in Antibes, during a farewell party for literary critic (and Algonquin Round Table member) Alexander Woollcott. After many toasts, "Zelda got up and said, 'I have been so touched by all these kind words. But what are words? Nobody has offered our departing heroes any gifts to take with them. I'll start off.' And she stepped out of her black lace panties and threw them toward Woollcott."

Of F. Scott, James Joyce succinctly noted, "He'll do himself an injury someday." Indeed, one night, there but for the grace of a farmer, they could have gotten themselves killed. F. Scott and Zelda were driving back to their villa after having dinner with the Murphys. For some reason, they drove their car out onto a train trestle and fell asleep. Luckily, the next morning a local farmer "saw them and pulled their car to safety a few minutes before the trolley was due."

How to sum it up? Nightclub owner Ada "Bricktop" Smith described her friend F. Scott as a "little boy in a man's body." John Dos Passos astutely added, "Like many drunks Scott took a malicious pleasure in making his friends uncomfortable." And Zelda? Perhaps she said it best herself, in a letter she wrote to F. Scott way back in 1919, when she said: "And I don't want to be famous and fêted—all I want is to be very young always and very irresponsible and to feel that my life is my own—to live and be happy and die in my own way to please myself."

THREE MILE LIMIT

1½ ounces brandy
¾ ounce light rum
1 teaspoon grenadine
1 dash fresh lemon juice

Shake well, then strain into a chilled cocktail glass.

Recipe from Barflies and Cocktails *(1927).*

LAW ENFORCEMENT DURING THE EARLY DAYS OF
Prohibition began at the so-called Three-Mile Limit, the outer
edge of America's territorial waters. This boundary stoked the imag-
inations of the more resourceful of our nation's entrepreneurs. In
short order, booze-bearing ships would drop anchor there, technically outside the reach of the law. Then, smaller boats would race out
to this so-called Rum Row or Rum Line, where transactions were
made, booze offloaded from the larger to the smaller craft, resulting
in a dash to the shore, to sell it to an on-shore bootlegger. Good old
American ingenuity, right?

The 1930 edition of Harry MacElhone's book *ABC of Mixing Cocktails* tells us that "this cocktail was invented at Harry's New York Bar,
Paris, by 'Chips' Brighton, the popular Bartender." It went on to say
that "one of the effects of the Volstead Act, people get busy when outside of the three miles."* Like I said, good old American ingenuity.

---

* US territorial waters would eventually be extended from three to twelve miles
out, see Twelve-Mile Cocktail (page 208).

One of the more notorious practitioners of the three-mile-limit trade was one William McCoy, a former shipbuilder based in South Florida who became something of a household name among rum-runners. That is, until he got the attention of the Coast Guard, which on November 23, 1923, dispatched the cutter *Seneca* to capture McCoy, his crew, and his ship, *Tomoka*. A spirited chase ensued, including several bursts fired from McCoy's deck-mounted machine gun. But after a few well-placed salvos from the *Seneca*'s far-larger, four-inch deck gun landed too close for comfort, McCoy agreed to surrender. After a few months in jail, McCoy retired on the millions he'd made as a rumrunner.

☞ **TASTING NOTE:** When made correctly, this is a solid, well-balanced drink. Just be judicious with the grenadine, you don't want it too sweet.

TOM AND JERRY

To make enough for ten drinks:

10 eggs
10 teaspoons sugar
20 ounces brandy
20 ounces Jamaican rum
20 ounces very hot or boiling water
Nutmeg, grated, for garnish

Break all the eggs and separate yolks from whites. Beat the whites "in such a manner that they become a stiff froth, then beat up the yolks until they are as thin as water." Blend the two back together, adding a teaspoon of sugar for each egg. Continue to stir until the mixture is a light batter. To make a drink, take two tablespoons of the batter, add two ounces each of brandy and rum, then fill the balance of a sturdy punch glass or mug with hot or boiling water. Stir well, top with grated nutmeg, and serve.

Recipe adapted from Barflies and Cocktails *(1927) and* ABC of Mixing Cocktails *(1930), both of which note that the drink is "a very popular beverage for Christmas or Birthday Parties."*

THE TOM AND JERRY IS A HISTORIC HOLIDAY DRINK. IT was invented in 1847 by the immortal Jerry Thomas, and appears in the earliest-known cocktail book, Thomas's *How to Mix Drinks, or The Bon Vivant's Companion* (1862). It seems that a customer asked Thomas for an egg beaten up in sugar, which got him thinking:

"How beautiful the egg and sugar would be with brandy to it!" Thomas implored his customer, "If you'll only bear with me for five minutes I'll fix you up a drink that'll do your heartstrings good." Jerry named the drink after himself, sort of; he had two pet white mice back in those days, Tom and Jerry. Indeed, to call the drink the "Jeremiah P. Thomas would have sounded rather heavy, and that wouldn't have done for a beverage," he explained.

Americans in 1920s Paris might have been more than happy to be abroad, but heartstrings being what they are, absence makes the heart grow fonder with thoughts of home, especially around the holidays. The Tom and Jerry had long been a fixture in wintertime Paris, going back to the nineteenth century. Writing on the topic of cold-weather drinks in Paris, one paper noted that "in the

Cover of the classic 1930 edition of ABC of Mixing Cocktails, *written by Harry MacElhone, owner of Harry's New York Bar.* IMAGE COURTESY OF EXPOSITION UNIVERSELLE DES VINS ET SPIRITUEUX.

American bar of the Café de la Paix the favorite hot drink seems to be a kind of Tom and Jerry." Knowing full well the appeal of a warming Yuletide drink, and wanting nothing more than to please its American clientele, Harry's New York Bar offered its patrons a complimentary glass of Tom and Jerry during the holidays.

Harry's is vividly described in *How to Wine and Dine in Paris* (1930):

> Harry's place has everything once familiar in America—a lipped mahogany bar . . . , a brass foot rail, a free lunch of pickles and cheese and crackers, all the usual hootch is on the shelf, several white-jacketed bartenders expert with cocktail shaker and full of pharmaceutical advice of a gray morning, swinging front doors, . . . a mahogany-framed bar mirror decorated frostily with soap at Christmas . . . and (also at that festive time) a big bowl of Tom-and-Jerry on the bar surrounded by China mugs—everything.

It's enough to make you want to run down rue Daunou shouting, "Merry Christmas, Bedford Falls!"

☞ **TASTING NOTE:** This is a great drink for a large crowd, as you can make a so-called "batter" and serve drinks individually as friends arrive. Since the original recipe called for Jamaica rum, try any of Appleton's fine darks, notably their Estate Signature Blend.

THE CAFÉ DE LA PAIX

Every major town seems to have its Café de la Paix, that obligatory destination where tourists are compelled to go, if only to tell their friends back home, yes, they went there. As *Paris with the Lid Lifted* told readers, "Hundreds of thousands of tourists pour into Paris each year. Every one of the 'hundreds of thousands' finds the Café de la Paix. They go to it, over and over again, and sprawl themselves out on the Terrace; order a three franc drink and sit and 'rubber' at the passersby for hours. On the most prominent corner in Paris, the Boulevard des Capucines and the Avenue de l'Opéra. The biggest restaurant building, the longest expanse of sidewalk tables, the greatest army of waiters, the most systematized service, the best coffee and the cheapest 'kill-time' spot in Paris. It is a tradition, that if you want to see anyone in Paris, and you sit in front of the Café de la Paix long enough, that person will pass."

163. PARIS — *Le Café de la Paix - Boulevard des Capucines*   A. P.
The Café de la Paix - Corner of the Opera

The immortal Café de la Paix.
VINTAGE POSTCARD FROM THE AUTHOR'S COLLECTION.

Donald Ogden Stewart's comical Americans-in-Paris novel *Mr. and Mrs. Haddock in Paris, France* echoes that theme, as Mr. Haddock enjoys "a tall glass of beautiful cold, foamy beer" on the terrace, saying, "I wish the boys could see me now." In his novel *Nineteen Nineteen*, John Dos Passos described a raucous Armistice celebration, much of it taking place at the Café de la Paix. And in Hemingway's short story "My Old Man," the café was a favorite hangout for the jockeys from the racecourse at Maisons-Laffitte: "I never really got to know Paris well, because I just came in about once or twice a week with the old man from Maisons and he always sat at the Café de la Paix on the Opera side with the rest of the gang from Maisons and I guess that's one of the busiest parts of the town."

And in spite of its touristy side, the café was also a part of the lives of some of the expatriates. In 1923, E. E. Cummings, Dos Passos, and Gilbert Seldes had "long bibulous and conversational dinners" there, and two years earlier, Ernest and Hadley Hemingway had their first Christmas dinner at Café de la Paix. To their chagrin, they didn't have enough money for the bill. While Hadley anxiously waited, Ernest had to race back to their flat on the Left Bank for more.

Although no longer "the cheapest 'kill-time' spot in Paris," spending an hour or two of an afternoon at the Café de la Paix remains a must on your Parisian to-do list.

TWELVE-MILE COCKTAIL

1 ounce light rum
½ ounce fresh lemon juice
½ ounce grenadine
½ ounce brandy
½ ounce rye whiskey

Shake well with ice, then strain into a chilled cocktail glass.

Recipe from Barflies and Cocktails *(1927).*

YET ANOTHER OF THE PROHIBITION-SPOOFING COCKTAILS at Harry's New York Bar* was the Twelve-Mile Cocktail. And how fitting that the drink named for an imaginary line on the high seas was invented by a man who was said to have "spent five years of his life on the ocean." That man would be globe-trotting journalist Tommy Millard, who is said to have held "the Pacific-crossing record for passengers. So many times, indeed, he long ago quit counting."

Consider this drink the partner-in-crime of the Three Mile Limit. See, in the early days of Prohibition, it was understood that the territorial waters of the United States (and its law enforcement) extended out three miles. This notion prompted a phenomenon known as the

---

* See also Three Mile Limit (page 201), Scoff-law Cocktail (page 179), and Volstead Cocktail (page 226).

Rum Line. Eventually, law enforcement began to flex its muscles, and three miles became twelve, and sometimes more. But why surround ourselves with all this water, let's get back to that drink.

If anyone were to create a drink to evoke the open seas, it had to be Millard, a true globe-trotter. You'd find him "in Shanghai, Timbuctoo [*sic*], London, Paris, Constantinople, New York, and San Francisco." Syndicated columnist O. O. McIntyre referred to him as "journalism's most persistent gadabout . . . He migrates between Shanghai and New York with side-trips to European capitals as casually as most New Yorkers ferry over to Staten Island." Millard covered the Greco-Turkish War, Boer War, Spanish-American War, Russo-Japanese War, and World War I. Through it all, Millard was quite the impeccable dresser. "A dandy, he carries a brace of wardrobe trunks that provide everything from full regalia for an embassy ball to tweedy togs for a hunt breakfast."

☛ **TASTING NOTE:** This is an excellent cocktail. It's a beautiful marriage of three spirits—rum, Cognac, and whiskey—which might ordinarily make one wary, but in this case they work quite well together.

VERMOUTH AND SELTZER

---

2 ounces vermouth (style depending on your taste)
3–4 ounces seltzer water
Orange wedge or lemon peel, for garnish

Fill a highball or a Collins glass with ice, add ingredients, stir, and garnish with orange wedge or lemon peel.

VERMOUTH IS ENJOYING A BIT OF A RENAISSANCE OF late, and that's a very good thing. It's the beneficiary of at least two trends: the broader craft-cocktail movement, and the popularity of "low-ABV" (alcohol-by-volume) drinks that can be enjoyed over the course of a long evening without causing (too much) impairment. As such, this and other vermouth and wine-based apéritifs were perfect in 1920s Paris, when the rigors of café society required many hours spent on the *terrasses* with a drink before you.

You'll find the Vermouth and Seltzer in one of Ernest Hemingway's earliest short stories, "My Old Man," from his 1923 collection, *Three Stories and Ten Poems*. It's the story of a father and son; the father is a jockey at Maisons-Laffitte, just outside Paris. The son is his faithful sidekick. The lower-calorie "vermouth and seltz" was a go-to drink for a weight-conscious jockey who . . .

> can't go boozing around because the trainer always has an eye on
> him. So mostly if a jock ain't working he sits around the Café de Paris

with the gang and they can all sit around about two or three hours in front of some drink like a vermouth and seltz and they talk and tell stories and shoot pool . . .

"My Old Man" is said to have been partly based on jockey Tod Sloan, who was one of the world's first sports celebrities. He dominated horse racing in England during the 1890s; by 1899, he'd won the majority of his races. He became too successful for his own good, and eventually lost his license when he was prosecuted for betting on himself. Other jockeys apparently did the same thing but were never charged. So what did he end up doing? He bought a joint in Paris called the New York Bar. In 1923, a Scot named Harry MacElhone bought it and renamed it Harry's New York Bar, and the rest, as they say, is history.

Perhaps this drink was a favorite of poet T. S. Eliot, who visited

Souvenir postcard from Maisons-Laffitte racetrack. FROM THE AUTHOR'S COLLECTION.

Paris (and his friend James Joyce) often. After all, in honor of that iconic brand of French vermouth, Eliot named his cat Noilly Prat!

☛ **TASTING NOTE:** The world of vermouth is exploding of late, opening up many new flavors and expressions with which to explore. Start with the classic brands, Dolin, Noilly Prat, Martini, Cinzano, Carpano et al., and branch out from there.

A DAY AT THE RACES

Paris in the 1920s was quite the racetrack town. Just outside Paris are such historic venues as Enghien, Auteuil, Maisons-Laffitte, Longchamp, Chantilly, Saint-Cloud, and others. *Paris with the Lid Lifted* encouraged tourists to go to the races on Sunday, and to "dress up for the Races as you would for a wedding," since "a Sunday at the Race Track is the dressiest occasion in Paris." Further, to really make a day of it, "the real way to go, is to hire a 7 passenger Rolls-Royce . . . You can swell up and make believe it is your own car."

But before you got dolled up and rented that Rolls, you'd want to spend some time at the bars most connected to the horse racing world. But they weren't near the track, they were closer to the Paris Opéra: Henry's Bar and the Hôtel Chatham bar, both located within steps of each other.

Henry's Bar (11 rue Volney at the corner of rue Daunou, also known as the Volney Club) opened in 1890 (only the Chatham was older) by one Henry Tépé, who is credited with introducing the American cocktail to Paris. It was described as

> another high class Clublike Rendezvous, but small and intimate. . . . Day after day, the same chaps come and spend the day. A great playground also for the Jockeys . . .

And for the high class Sporting Man and Man of Leisure, about Paris. Actually, an Exclusive Club.

Basil Woon reinforced the "Exclusive Club" comment, noting that "anyone can walk into Henry's bar, but only a select few can get a smile out of Ernest or John, the two bartenders. There may be a roaring fire in the anthracite stove, but the stranger strolling into Henry's for the first time needs his coat-collar well turned up to ward off the chill."

HENRY'S HOTEL, II, Rue Volney."— PARIS   Téléphone : 247.86

Vintage postcard from Henry's Hotel, showing the barroom.
FROM THE AUTHOR'S COLLECTION.

Meanwhile, the Hôtel Chatham's bar, just down the street at 17–19 rue Daunou, also attracted the racetrack touts. And that's not all it had in common with Henry's:

> Of the other bars, the Chatham like Henry's is not the most homelike place in the world for the stranger. It is largely crowded with race-track people-jockeys, trainers, book-makers and hangers-on. The Chatham is the oldest "American" bar in Europe.

There's one other place you might have wanted to hit to get a hot tip; that would be over in Montparnasse, at the Sélect, where Harold Stearns held court. He had a gig with the Paris edition of the *Chicago Tribune* as "Peter Pickem," and to quote Robert McAlmon, Stearns "picked the winners at the racecourse at Maisons-Laffitte (or else failed to pick them)."

A noted intellectual and writer, "Stearns left for Paris on 4 July, 1921, after delivering his book *Civilization in the United States* to his publisher." His parting quote might be one of the best things he ever wrote: "I'm going to Paris, . . . I'll meet you on the Left Bank. I'll drink your health and good red Burgundy, I'll kiss all the girls for you. I'm sick of this country. I'm going abroad to write one good novel." Legendary barman Jimmie Charters summed up ol' Harold pretty well as "the man who preferred to be a racehorse expert rather than (perhaps) a great writer."

Ernest Hemingway included Stearns in his 1926 novel, *The Sun Also Rises*, as the character Harvey Stone, sitting at the Sélect with "a pile of saucers in front of him, and he needed a shave." In another scene you'll find him at Harry's New York Bar, where Jake Barnes allows the flat-broke Stone to win two hundred francs off him rolling dice.

One such "hot tip" that Harold gave proved somewhat disastrous for John Dos Passos and Hemingway. Said Dos Passos: "We got our tips free from Harold Stearns. Harold . . . gave up writing and dropped everything. Even his pursuit of drink and women seemed to lack conviction. . . . He lived a pathetic barfly life eking out a living selling tips on ponies to American tourists he picked up in the various gin mills he frequented."

It seems there was a "plush steeplechase" race, and Stearns gave them a hot tip on a long shot. Dos and Hem scraped up "several hundred francs and made for the track." Visions of "a bangup meal at Foyot's" after the victory danced in their heads. Well, it didn't go exactly according to plan:

The horse was a jumper all right but at the water jump he balked, threw his jockey over his head and bolted back round the track the wrong way. He took a lot of jumps backward before he was caught. The race was a shambles. We nearly died laughing. I went back to Paris with my convictions about the folly of gambling much fortified. Next time we went to Henry's bar Harold pretended not to see us.

And you wondered why Hemingway chose to lampoon his friends in *The Sun Also Rises*.

VERMOUTH CASSIS / CHAMBÉRY CASSIS

---

3 ounces Chambéry (dry) vermouth
½ ounce crème de cassis liqueur or currant syrup
1–2 ounces seltzer water, to taste

Fill a highball or Collins glass with ice, add ingredients, stir well.

Recipe from The Artistry of Mixing Drinks *(1936).*

THIS DELICIOUS DRINK IS KNOWN BY SEVERAL NAMES: Chambéry cassis, Vermouth Cassis, Export Cassis, not to mention the *Pompier*, the French term for "fireman," as it was popular with that profession. With sweet vermouth it becomes the Cascade Highball, the Cinzano Cassis, or the Turin-Cassis. Under whichever name, it's a tall drink made with dry vermouth and crème de cassis, a sweet black currant liqueur primarily made in the Burgundy region of France,* but sometimes made with currant syrup. If you were to order one at a 1920s Paris café, it might be a do-it-yourself affair: "The waiter brings a goblet, Vermouth, black currant syrup, ice, and a siphon, and the mixture is made according to taste."

The drink is found often in magazines and guidebooks, biographies and in prose. In 1923, *Time* magazine noted that the drink "is slightly sweet and deliciously tart. In France it is popular enough to

---

* See Vin Blanc Cassis (page 224).

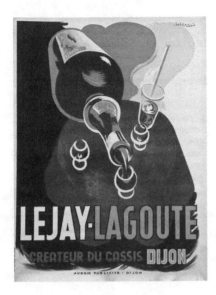

Vintage Lejay crème de cassis ad. IMAGE COURTESY OF MAISON LEJAY LAGOUTE.

warrant a seat in the Chamber of Deputies." In 1934, *House & Garden* added that "the Vermouth Cassis is as much a part of Paris as the Bois." John Dos Passos would occasionally meet Hemingway at Closerie des Lilas "to drink such innocuous fluid as vermouth cassis while we talked about the difficulties of putting things down on paper."

Poet Allen Tate also recalled having a Vermouth Cassis one afternoon in 1929 with Ernest Hemingway, but this time it was the Café Voltaire (1 place de l'Odeon), and this time it wasn't so pleasant. It seems they got into a discussion over the extent to which Hemingway was influenced by (or indebted to) Daniel Defoe and Frederick Marryat, and Tate walked away concluding that Hemingway was a "complete son of a bitch."

Jean Rhys also has one of her characters drinking the Vermouth Cassis in her semiautobiographical 1928 novel, *Quartet.* "'Encore deux vermouth-cassis!' said Mr. Heidler to the waitress." *Quartet* was loosely based on her affair with English novelist and publisher Ford

Madox Ford (with Mr. Heidler as Ford). So, it makes sense Hemingway mentioned the drink in his Paris memoir, *A Moveable Feast*, in a chapter concerning, you guessed it, Ford. In the comical chapter "Ford Madox Ford and the Devil's Disciple," Hemingway was at the Closerie des Lilas, "the nearest good café" to his flat on 113 rue Notre-Dame-des-Champs. He often went there to write, to warm up, and to escape from the noises of his young son, Bumby. Hemingway sat there alone, enjoying the coming of evening, "watching the light change on the trees and the buildings and the passage of the great slow horses of the outer boulevard." Ford's intrusion all but ruined the evening.

Despite Ford's role in helping his career (in 1924 he hired him to assist in editing the *Transatlantic Review*), Hemingway had little tolerance for him. On this evening, he recalled Ford as "breathing

Hemingway's "home café," the Closerie des Lilas, at the corner of boulevards Montparnasse and Saint-Michel, 1924. PHOTOGRAPH COURTESY OF THE BIBLIOTHÈQUE NATIONALE DE FRANCE.

heavily through a heavy, stained mustache," his breath "fouler than the spout of any whale." He feared that Ford's breath would "foul" the taste of his drink, but since it was an open-air café, "it still tasted very good." Hemingway felt obliged to invite him to join him for a drink. Initially, Ford ordered a Chambéry Cassis, but then changed his mind to a *Fine à l'Eau* (Cognac and water).

When the waiter returned with the *Fine à l'Eau*, Ford corrected him.

"It wasn't a brandy and soda," he said helpfully but severely. "I ordered a Chambéry vermouth and Cassis."

"It's all right, Jean," Hemingway says. "I'll take the *fine*. Bring Monsieur what he orders now."

"What I ordered," corrected Ford.

In the chapter titled "Secret Pleasures," Hemingway recounted his decision to leave the *Toronto Daily Star* and focus on his prose writing. After this momentous decision, they decided to "have a Chambéry Cassis to celebrate," with Hadley noting that "it's a part of being free from all that awfulness."

The Chambéry Cassis also played a role in Hemingway's personal life, in the wake of his breakup with Hadley in the winter of 1926–27. Hemingway stayed in Gerald Murphy's studio apartment on rue Froidevaux. Living alone, feeling sorry for himself, he dined each day at a café called the Three Musketeers. "Ernest would walk into the café slowly, self-consciously, and select a table close to the windows. . . . Ernest would usually order a vermouth cassis, and when the waiter would bring it, Ernest would squirt 'charged water into the glass so that the vivid color paled and the glass filled.' Ernest would taste his drink, and, before he ordered his food, look out the window for awhile. Under the drink was a saucer with the price of the drink as part of the design. Each cassis cost Ernest two francs—little enough for a 'ticket that entitled him to stay as long as he wished in the warmth of the café.'"

☛ **TASTING NOTE:** This is a refreshing low-alcohol drink, with subtle and sweet flavors of the crème de cassis marrying well with the complex flavors of the vermouth. Dolin Dry or Blanc are fine choices for vermouth, and for the cassis go with Mathilde Liqueur or Lejay.

VERMOUTH COCKTAIL

2 ounces sweet vermouth
2 ounces dry vermouth
2 dashes Angostura aromatic bitters
2 dashes orange bitters
Lemon wedge or peel

Shake well, then strain into a chilled cocktail glass, squeeze a lemon wedge or peel atop the drink.

Recipe from Barflies and Cocktails *(1927).*

THE EMERGENCE OF VERMOUTH REVOLUTIONIZED THE bartending world.* Although it wasn't formally introduced to old man whiskey until the mid 1870s, the Vermouth Cocktail, a simple mix of vermouth and bitters, appeared in cocktail books as early as 1869.

The Vermouth Cocktail joined other low-alcohol drinks like the Vermouth and Seltzer, the Chambéry Cassis, the Vin Blanc Cassis, the Champagne Cocktail, and the Mimosa as being very popular in 1920s Paris for those who were, as the old beer jingle went, "having more than one." You'll find it in many of the popular bartending books of the day, and in works of fiction. For example, in F. Scott Fitzgerald's 1934 novel, *Tender Is the Night*, Dick and Nicole Diver, "as

---

* See the Manhattan (page 130).

fine-looking a couple as could be found in Paris," enjoyed "a vermouth and bitters in the shadow by Fouquet's bar."

Salvador Dalí also loved vermouth. In his autobiography, he succinctly expressed the impact that vermouth and olives (which he adored) might have had on his circle of artists:

> The double vermouths with olives contributed generously to crystallize this budding "post-war" confusion, by bringing a dose of poorly dissimulated sentimentalism which was the element most propitious to the elusive transmutations of heroism, bad faith, coarse elegance and hyperchloridic digestions, all mixed up with anti-patriotism; and from this whole amalgam a hatred rooted in bourgeois mentality which was destined to make headway grew, waxed rich, opening up new branches daily, backed by unlimited credit, until the day of the famous crash of the then distant Civil War.

Don't look now, but I think the clock on the wall just melted.

Ernest Hemingway also developed a taste for the drink during his Paris years, and took it with him to Key West when he formally moved there in 1931. In an *Esquire* article, he told of a fishing trip out on the Gulf Stream, enjoying "tall glasses with mixed French and Italian vermouth (two parts of French to one of Italian, with a dash of bitters and a lemon peel, fill glass with ice, stir and serve)."

And for a truly French Caribbean variation on this classic, try the Martinican Vermouth Cocktail, which, depending on your perspective, is a rhum Manhattan or rhum Vermouth Cocktail. The drink made its debut in the influential 1896 book *Bariana* by Louis Fouquet. Here's how:

MARTINICAN VERMOUTH COCKTAIL

1½ ounces Martinique rhum
1½ ounces sweet vermouth
2 dashes Angostura aromatic bitters
2 dashes orange curaçao
2 dashes crème de noyaux
1 teaspoon pineapple syrup
Lemon peel, for garnish

Shake well with ice, then strain into a chilled cocktail glass, garnish with lemon peel.

This might actually be the best drink in my entire book. Sadly, Fouquet died of typhoid in 1905, otherwise I'd like to think both he and this drink would have a more lasting legacy. The drink was still being made in 1920s France, as it appears in the 1927 book *900 Recettes de Cocktails et Boissons Americaines*. With the pineapple and rum combination, this drink has a distinct Tiki feel to it, even though that era was launched forty years later.

☛ **TASTING NOTE:** The Vermouth Cocktail is a delicious drink, and may change how you think about vermouth, as you can vary the expressions of vermouth as well as the bitters. If you're making the Martinican Vermouth Cocktail, pineapple juice works well if you can't find pineapple syrup (add a little simple syrup if it's too tart). For the noyaux, Tempus Fugit or Noyau de Poissy are both recommended.

VIN BLANC CASSIS
(Now Known as Kir)

---

4 ounces chilled dry white wine
1 ounce chilled crème de cassis
Red fruit, for garnish

Serve in a Champagne flute, garnish with any red fruit, such as a raspberry or strawberry.

❖

KIR ROYALE

4 ounces chilled dry Champagne or sparkling wine
1 ounce chilled crème de cassis
Serve in a Champagne flute, garnish with any red fruit, such as a raspberry or strawberry.

THESE DRINKS ARE ESSENTIALLY IDENTICAL; KIR IS MADE with a still wine (traditionally, a dry white Burgundy known as Aligoté), and Kir Royale is made with a sparkling wine, such as Champagne. Prior to the 1960s, it was known as Vin Blanc Cassis (or just Blanc Cassis), and it was especially popular in Burgundy. During World War II, a Catholic priest by the name of Félix Kir served illustriously with the French Resistance, playing a key role in the liberation of some five thousand French prisoners of war being held by the Nazis at the Longvic Prison, near Dijon. Kir was later elected mayor of Dijon. The residents of Burgundy were so devoted to him that they eventually renamed their cherished regional drink after him.

Novelist Henry Miller was a fan of the Vin Blanc Cassis, as well as *Fine à l'Eau*, and often enjoyed them at the Bouquet d'Alésia. Miller later wrote, "Hardly a day of my life, after moving to the Villa Seurat, ever passed without a drink or two at either Café Zeyer or the Café Bouquet d'Alésia."

John Dos Passos wrote of summer days at Sara and Gerald Murphy's Cap d'Antibes retreat Villa America, recalling "the blue flare of the Mediterranean noon, and the taste of vin de Cassis in the briney Mediterranean breeze."

These two drinks are among the classic, low-alcohol wine/vermouth-based apéritif drinks of France that were very popular from the nineteenth century onward, and remain so today.

☛ **TASTING NOTE:** Ratios vary: more crème de cassis will make for a sweeter drink. Further, you can alter the sweetness by using a drier or sweeter sparkling wine. And don't skimp on the crème de cassis; avoid those mass-produced bottles on the bottom shelf. Go with Lejay or Mathilde Liqueur.

VOLSTEAD COCKTAIL

> **1 ounce rye whiskey**
> **1 ounce Swedish punsch**
> **½ ounce fresh orange juice**
> **½ ounce raspberry syrup**
> **1 dash anisette**
> **Orange peel, for garnish (optional)**
>
> ---
>
> Shake well with ice, then strain into a chilled cocktail glass. Garnish optional—an orange peel is nice.
>
> *Recipe from* Barflies and Cocktails *(1927).*

IN THAT GREAT AMERICAN TRADITION OF POPULAR dissent, Harry's New York Bar featured at least four cocktails lampooning Prohibition.* According to *Barflies and Cocktails,* "This cocktail was invented at the Harry's New York Bar, Paris, in honour of Mr. Andrew J. Volstead, who brought out the Dry Act in U.S.A. and was the means of sending to Europe such large numbers of Americans to quench their thirst."

Harry MacElhone was a Scot, but he had a keen awareness of the commercial benefits of offering an oasis for Yanks in Paris. By its name, its furnishings, its solid American cocktails, and its promotion, Harry's was a home away from home. Harry's ads were

---

* See also the Scoff-law Cocktail (page 179), the Three Mile Limit (page 201), and the Twelve-Mile Cocktail (page 208).

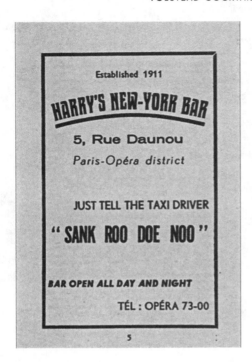

Advertisement for Harry's, found within the bartending book ABC of Mixing Cocktails *(1934).* IMAGE COURTESY OF COLLECTIF1806.COM.

designed to reel in those new arrivals (they made it simple, "Just tell the taxi driver, '*sank roo doe noo*,'" the bastardized phonetical equivalent of *cinc* (as in "5") *rue Daunou*). "Harry's Bar, at 5 o'clock, is typical of the corner of 42nd Street and Broadway, New York, 20 years ago," one guidebook proclaimed, "something to bring tears to the eyes of a sentimentalist during Prohibition."

This drink is a good introduction to Swedish punsch, a sugar cane-based liqueur, popular in Scandinavia for centuries. It was largely forgotten after Prohibition, however Kronan's launch in 2012 has helped revive the category. It can be enjoyed by itself, as well as within cocktails.

☞ **TASTING NOTE:** Consider cutting the raspberry syrup by at least half (Monin works well); you can always add more but you can't take it out. Kronan Swedish Punsch is highly recommended. This drink is a good example of how anise or anisette can be used as a flavor enhancer. Victor "Trader Vic" Bergeron was known to use Pernod in this manner in a number of his classic Tiki drinks.

WHISKEY AND SODA

2 ounces whiskey (your choice: Scotch, rye, bourbon,
Canadian, et cetera)*
4 ounces seltzer water
Lemon or lime wedge (or peel), for garnish

Fill a highball glass with ice, add ingredients, stir, serve. Option, garnish with a wedge (or peel) of lemon or lime.

F YOU'VE EVER WONDERED WHAT A "HIGHBALL" IS, THIS is likely the original. The term describes an easy to make combination of a distilled spirit and a nonalcoholic, carbonated beverage, such as tonic water, seltzer, cola, or ginger ale. It was said to have been invented by Patrick Gavin Duffy in the 1890s at the Ashland House in New York City.

This drink was popular among the Anglo-American expat crowd in 1920s Paris. Jimmie Charters tells a funny story about it. A man came into the bar and ordered a Whiskey and Soda, "And make it strong, Jimmie! I need a strong one before the big fight!" he says. After he'd had more than a few "in rapid succession," all of which to prepare him for "the big fight," Jimmie finally asked when and where this "big fight" will be, for he'd like to watch it. Comes the reply: "Oh, you'll see it all right, because it's going to take place right now between you and me when you find out I have no money to pay!"

---

* "Whiskey" tends to suggest Irish or American whiskey, while "whisky" suggests Scotch, though exceptions, such as Maker's Mark, abound.

Great American composer George Gershwin was a Scotch and Soda man, and if you'll believe the folklore of Harry's New York Bar, Gershwin composed *An American in Paris* on the piano of Harry's downstairs cabaret. While the story might be a myth, it is true that he used the sound of Paris taxicabs in his score.

While it was Champagne that Ernest Hemingway and F. Scott Fitzgerald drank during their first meeting at the Dingo, in April 1925 (and F. Scott was "overserved"), he fared better the second time, at Closerie des Lilas. "On this day as we sat outside on the terrace of the Lilas and we watched it get dusk and the people passing on the sidewalk and the thin grey light of the evening changing, there was no chemical change in him from the two whiskey and sodas that we drank." Indeed, this appears to have been Hemingway's go-to drink at Lilas; in *A Moveable Feast* he speaks of having a few with poet Evan Shipman. Their waiter, Jean, had become disgruntled when management told him he had to shave his cherished mustache. It seems they were installing an "American bar" and wanted to attract a classier clientele. In protest, Jean "used no measuring glass and poured the whiskey until the glass was more than three-quarters full." Shipman, having enjoyed the fruits of Jean's "stick-it-to-the-man" act before, counseled: "Take the first sip very carefully, Hem. Properly handled, they will hold us for some time." Shipman later quipped, "It's a good thing Dostoyevsky didn't know Jean, he might have died of drink."

A deleted scene from the original manuscript of *The Sun Also Rises* suggests that Hemingway and John Dos Passos were also beneficiaries to the waiter's largesse. "At that time, a fellow named Dos Passos was in town and we were accustomed to go and drink in the cool of the evenings at a place called the Closerie des Lilas . . . where we knew a waiter who would give us two whiskeys for the price of one whiskey owing to the dislike he had for his boss."

Throughout his life, Hemingway complained bitterly about being "bitched" by interruptions—phone calls, friends, et cetera. "I have to have enforced discipline or I just don't get any writing done," he noted in 1946. "The trouble is I like to see people, and a writer doesn't have an office organization to protect him from friends the way a business man does." In *The Sun Also Rises*, Jake Barnes used the Whiskey and Soda to get out of such social entanglements. When Robert Cohn dropped by Jake's office uninvited, Jake suggested they have a drink at the café downstairs. His plan: "Go have a drink with them, then say, 'Well, I've got to get back and get off some cables,' and it was done. It is very important to discover graceful exits like that in the newspaper business, where it is such an important part of the ethics that you should never seem to be working." So Jake and Robert went to a nearby café for a Whiskey and Soda.

Interestingly enough, Harold Loeb, on whom Robert Cohn's character was based, was also drinking a Whiskey and Soda when he first met Duff Twysden (the real-life Lady Brett Ashley) at the Sélect. They then arranged to have their first rendezvous at the Falstaff, and only Jimmy was present. They could count on his discretion "because he was such a good chap."

One evening at the Sélect, artists Chaïm Soutine and Jules Pascin, the latter being known for his nudes, were having "ten whiskeys each." Soutine mischievously said to Pascin, "Don't think that I don't appreciate your paintings. Your girls excite me." Pascin brusquely replied, "I forbid you to excite yourself in front of my women!"

Fitzgerald has his character Dick Diver ordering a "Blackenwite with siphon" at the Hôtel Carleton, "Black & White" being a popular brand of blended Scotch whisky. The waiter informs him in French that there is no more Black & White, they have only "le Johnny Walkair,"* to which Diver replies, "*Ça va*," as in "it's okay."

Hemingway also included the Whiskey and Soda in his 1929 classic, *A Farewell to Arms*. Frederic Henry has defected from World War I and has run away with his lover, Catherine. Henry ordered a Whiskey and Soda from the hotel's room service. As he "poured the soda slowly over the ice into the whiskey," he reflected that "good whiskey was very pleasant. It was one of the pleasant parts of life."

---

* Implying Johnnie Walker, but with the French accent.

☛ **TASTING NOTE:** The world of whiskey is exploding with craft distilleries popping up all over. This classic offers a chance to play around with this ever-increasing palate of flavors and expressions.

WHISKEY SOUR
(Citron Pressé and Whiskey)

1½ ounces whiskey (your choice, Scotch, rye,
Bourbon, Canadian, et cetera)
½ ounce fresh lemon juice
½–¾ ounce simple syrup
Lemon peel, for garnish

Shake well, then strain into a chilled cocktail glass. Garnish with a lemon peel.

THIS IS A CLASSIC DRINK, AND THE "SOUR" IS ONE OF the more important categories of cocktails. In my view, if you can master the sour, you can not only make a wide range of drinks but also use that simple platform to create new ones. This simple construct of sweet, sour, and strong is the basis for other classics such as the Margarita, the Daiquiri, the Jack Rose, the Pisco Sour, and many others. They're all essentially the same drink with different components swapped out for each other.

In his Paris memoir, *A Moveable Feast*, Ernest Hemingway writes at length about his relationship with F. Scott Fitzgerald. He tells of their

234 · A DRINKABLE FEAST

first meeting in the spring of 1925,* at the Dingo Bar, where Heming-
way was "sitting with some completely worthless characters," namely
Duff Twysden and Pat Guthrie, on whom Brett Ashley and Mike
Campbell in *The Sun Also Rises* were based. Behind the bar was leg-
endary barman Jimmie Charters. And if this didn't already sound
like a who's who of 1920s expat Paris, in walked F. Scott Fitzgerald.
Hemingway knew of F. Scott; he was already a successful writer, and
The Great Gatsby had just been released.

As it happened, F. Scott overindulged at that first meeting and
passed out. Hemingway came to learn that this was simply a "thing"
for both F. Scott and Zelda. "Becoming unconscious when they drank
had always been their great defense," Hemingway noted. It wouldn't
take much drinking for them to "go to sleep like children . . . and when
they woke they will be fresh and happy, not having taken enough
alcohol to damage their bodies before it made them unconscious."

They met again a few days later at the Closerie des Lilas. Here,
F. Scott asked Ernest a favor. F. Scott and Zelda's Renault motor car
had been left "in Lyon because of bad weather," and would Hem be
good enough to help F. Scott retrieve it? They could ride down together on the train, get the car, and then drive it back to Paris.
Hemingway thought it a fine idea, as it would give him a chance to
spend time with a more accomplished writer.

The trip was a debacle, something to laugh about years later, perhaps. Or write about. In Lyon, Hemingway was "astonished to find
that the small Renault had no top." See, F. Scott and Zelda had been
"compelled" to ditch it in Lyon because she'd ordered the top to be
cut off after a minor accident in Marseille. She liked convertibles,
anyway, it seemed. So, F. Scott and Hem started off for Paris in their
topless French car.

Unfortunately, they "were halted by rain about an hour north of
Lyon," and "were halted by rain possibly ten times." Along the way,
they ate an excellent lunch of truffled roast chicken, washed down

---

* In the book *Exiles from Paradise: Zelda and Scott Fitzgerald,* Zelda's friend Sara
Mayfield states that their introduction at the Dingo was arranged by Donald
Ogden Stewart.

with white Mâcon wine. They bought several bottles, which Hemingway "uncorked as we needed them." Drinking wine straight from the bottle was particularly exciting for F. Scott, "as though he were slumming or as a girl might be excited by going swimming for the first time without a bathing suit."

But the fun soon ended the wetter they got; F. Scott feared that he'd contracted congestion of the lungs, and he insisted that they stop at the next town before "the onset of the fever and delirium." Hemingway hoped that a few more swigs of the Mâcon might make F. Scott

F. Scott, Zelda, and Scottie Fitzgerald in their Renault KJ in front of the Enrico Toti statue in Rome, Italy. The Renault would provide the vehicle (literally and figuratively) for Hemingway and Fitzgerald's Lyon-to-Paris misadventures. The folding convertible top can be shown on the rear of the car; this photo was apparently taken before Zelda had it removed. PHOTOGRAPH COURTESY OF THE F. SCOTT FITZGERALD PAPERS, PRINCETON UNIVERSITY LIBRARY, WITH THE PERMISSION OF THE TRUSTEES OF THE FITZGERALD ESTATE UNDER AGREEMENT DATED JULY 3, 1975. CREATED BY FRANCES SCOTT FITZGERALD SMITH.

feel better since, after all, "a good white wine, moderately full-bodied but with a low alcoholic content, was almost a specific against the disease." His father was a physician, after all.

They finally found a hotel in Chalon-sur-Saône, and F. Scott took to bed. Hemingway became doctor and nurse, and while their rain-soaked clothing dried, he ordered "two *citron pressés* and two double whiskies," which F. Scott dismissed as one of "those old wives' remedies." Hemingway tried to order a full bottle but they only sold it by the drink. F. Scott soon revealed himself to be an insufferable hypochondriac, demanding aspirin and a thermometer. Eventually the hotel waiter brought both, however the thermometer was intended for measuring bathwater (it had "a wooden back and enough metal to sink it in the bath"). Hemingway "shook the thermometer down professionally" and wryly said, 'You're lucky it's not a rectal thermometer."

He took F. Scott's temperature under his arm, and somehow convinced him that 37.6 degrees Celsius (99.7 degrees Fahrenheit) was normal. F. Scott insisted that Hemingway take his own temperature, which he did, reporting the exact same number. "I was trying to remember whether thirty-seven six was really normal or not," Hemingway recalled. "It did not matter, for the thermometer, unaffected, was steady at thirty."

"Scott drank the whisky sour down very fast now and asked me to order another." Which Hemingway did. They soon went down to the hotel restaurant, where they had a carafe of Fleurie (a dry, light red from Beaujolais) with their snails, followed by a bottle of Montagny, "a light, pleasant white wine of the neighborhood," with their main course, *poularde de Bresse.* And then, F. Scott did what he often did: he passed out, "with his head on his hands. It was natural and there was no theater about it and it even looked as though he were careful not to spill or break things." Hemingway and the waiter got him back upstairs to bed, and Hemingway went back down and finished the dinner (and the wine).

The next day they drove back to Paris, the weather was beautiful, "the air freshly washed and the hills and the field and the vineyards all new." He said his goodbyes to F. Scott, and Hemingway returned to his apartment. Happy to be back home, Hemingway and Hadley celebrated with a drink at the Closerie des Lilas. He told Hadley that he'd learned one thing, "Never to go on trips with anyone you do not love."

A final note on the Whiskey Sour, Harry MacElhone was quoted in 1951 as saying he missed the good old days when Hemingway and Fitzgerald were customers, and that "Hemingway could down 20 whiskey sours at one sitting and then go back to his hotel to work." I'm a little dubious of this story, but it comes with the territory.

☞ **TASTING NOTE:** Use whichever whiskey you want, be it Bourbon, rye, Scotch, Canadian, Japanese, et cetera. This drink works well on the rocks or up, your call. You can make it as a classic sour, measuring whiskey, lemon juice, and sugar/simple syrup, or just add whiskey to homemade lemonade, as it seems Hem and F. Scott did.

END OF THE ERA

ALL GREAT EPOCHS MUST COME TO AN END, AND *les années folles* was no exception. Many of the reasons for the migration *to* Paris contributed to the exodus *from* it. First off, the ridiculously favorable exchange rate could not last forever, and the more people who came to Paris, particularly in the arts colony of Montparnasse, the more these newcomers made the place less desirable to the old guard. Its timing was in the eye of the beholder. To bartender Jimmie Charters, it was gradual then abrupt. "Montparnasse really ended in 1929 with the beginning of the Depression in America, but as an artist colony it had been on the wane for some time before that." Jimmie observed that "when the sightseers . . . and tourists descended on the Quarter . . . the artists and writers began to move out. . . . Then came the crash, and most of these new customers were forced to return home, leaving behind only a few diehards who literally could not tear themselves away from the scene of past glories."

Nightclub owner Jed Kiley agreed: "In November of 1929 the big Depression bounced off of Wall Street and hit Paris hard. It was a TKO for the American Colony. Every Yank who had ever been spending money like water suddenly went dry. They had it one day and didn't have it the next."

Hemingway had his own "end of an era" indicators. "Although

nobody knows when they start everybody is pretty sure when they are over and when, in one year, Kiki became monumental and Montparnasse became rich, prosperous, brightly lighted, . . . and they sold caviar at the Dôme, well, the Era, for what it was worth, and personally I don't think it was worth much, was over."

Some participants relished the golden days, while some licked their wounds. F. Scott Fitzgerald offered some poignant observations in his prose,* which spoke of the wild past and the damage done. This is a recurring theme in "Babylon Revisited." In one scene, Charlie (the protagonist) visits "Bricktop's, where he had parted with so many hours and so much money." In another scene, when dining with his young daughter, Charlie specifically chose "Le Grand Vatel, the only restaurant he could think of not reminiscent of champagne dinners and long luncheons that began at two and ended in a blurred and vague twilight." He had earlier visited a cherished old haunt, the Hotel Ritz, but felt starkly out of place. "The stillness in the Ritz bar was strange and portentous. It was not an American bar anymore—he felt polite in it, and not as if he owned it. It had gone back into France. He felt the stillness from the moment he got out of the taxi."

A 1939 newspaper story echoed this theme, complaining that at "Harry's Bar, gathering place for years of the visiting American clans, now has more French patrons than Americans or British."

Laurence Vail, husband to heiress Peggy Guggenheim, also pined for the glory days, and dismissed the new denizens of Montparnasse as poseurs. They "sit for hours over two bocks, one quart Vichy, and three grenadines. A morose contrast to the days when, in less than two hours, Flossie Martin and other notables could pile towers of saucers half a meter high." For her part, Flossie would later reminisce to Malcolm Cowley how she yearned to be "just sitting outside the Sélect with a good long drink and nothing to do but drink it." When facing the end of that brilliant era, writer Kay Boyle shrugged and said, "There was nothing to do except have one more drink."

---

* Notably in his novel *Tender Is the Night,* and the short stories "One Trip Abroad" and "Babylon Revisited."

Author and diarist Anaïs Nin fondly recalled the camaraderie of the arts colony, calling it "a patina of shared lives." Hemingway famously ended his memoir, *A Moveable Feast*, by concluding:

> There is never any ending to Paris, and the memory of each person who has lived in it differs from that of any other. We always returned to it no matter who we were or how it was changed or with what difficulties, or ease, it could be reached. Paris was always worth it and you received return for whatever you brought to it.

These final two quotes speak for themselves:

"It was a useless silly life—and I have missed it every day since."
—HAROLD STEARNS

"One's an ass to leave Paris." —LADY BRETT ASHLEY, *The Sun Also Rises*

NOTABLE QUOTES ABOUT 1920S PARIS, DRINKS, OR BOTH

FOR YOUR ENJOYMENT, WHAT FOLLOWS IS A COLLECTION of commentaries on Paris during *les années folles.*

"There is an atmosphere of spiritual effort here. No other city is quite like it. It is a racecourse tension. I wake early, often at five o'clock, and start writing at once." —JAMES JOYCE

"What lured us to Paris and held us there . . . was . . . the magnificent work being done by people from all over the world and in all the arts. . . . There were a lot of fakes, a lot of phonies, and there undoubtedly were people who had come as refugees, exiles. But what I remember are the individual human beings who I had the luck to know. The people who were good seemed to respond to that fever of greatness by becoming great themselves." —ARCHIBALD MACLEISH

"You can drink some of the cocktails all of the time and all of the cocktails some of the time, but—think it over, Judy."
—F. SCOTT FITZGERALD's inscription in a book given to a friend

"So many thousands of people from all over the world found self-expression of one kind or another in a general release from inhibitions—the greatest wild-oat field the world has ever known!"
—JIMMIE CHARTERS

"That Raspail and Montparnasse corner would light up brightly with the cafés crowded and the headwaiters shaking hands with the regular patrons. Or down at the Deux Magots I could see Fitzgerald coming to meet me with his elegant and distinguished air. And in the oak-paneled Falstaff, Jimmy behind the bar, and Hemingway coming in, looking lonely, then his face lighting up with his quick sweet smile when he saw us . . ." —MORLEY CALLAGHAN

"It was a fine place to be quite young in and it is a necessary part of a man's education. We all loved it once and we lie if we say we didn't. But she is like a mistress who does not grow old and she has other lovers now. She was old to start with but we did not know it then. We thought she was just older than we were, and that was attractive then. So when we did not love her any more we held it against her. But that was wrong because she is always the same age and she always has new lovers." —ERNEST HEMINGWAY

"In terms of just plain feeling good, France was in those days, even for the poor, the richest life an artist ever knew." —VIRGIL THOMSON

"Upon arriving there after an absence, I was always in a fever of excitement, and couldn't do quickly enough the bars of Montparnasse and the cabarets of Montmartre, and the Champs Elysées district. . . . Crossing the Seine into the Place de la Concorde on a misty spring morning, or seeing Notre Dame des Champs from river level at dawn, when well on with drink, still brought a foaming ecstasy into me, a stroke of lightning to the heart or mind about the wonder of it." —ROBERT MCALMON

"Paris is a real land of enchantment—a continual, dizzy, giddy joyride—different, dazzling, novel, colorful, bizarre, panoramic, kaleidoscopic, chic, charming, and utterly Foreign. Foreign from the 'toot-toot' of the taxi horn to the tidy, tippling tables of the Terrace Cafés; from the astounding, startling sidewalk Bungalow-Lavatories, to the red-bearded, Beret-topped, wasp-waisted native

Boulevardier—a thrill, a tingle, a tickle a second, in Paris. Paris whirls. Your brain whirls. It is Cocktail after Cocktail; cocotte after cocotte; cabaret after cabaret; dawn after dawn; thrill after thrill; adventure after adventure; headache after headache; bromo after bromo. You will want to kick holes in the sky and bite the stars; take in the Sun and shine up the Moon—in Paris. And that is exactly what you are going to do. But keep in step and keep sober and don't balk at anything. Go where you are told to go and you will see every little nook and cranny of Paris that there is to see, and you will get a hundred franc return on every single franc you spend. You will just have the time of your life." —BRUCE REYNOLDS

"I have always thought that the Americans and English in the quarter—women and men—could be placed into one of three groups: first, those serious people, principally writers and artists, who worked all day and played in the early evening, and perhaps also on weekends; second, those who worked a little, played rather hard, and made love with serious intent; and then the others, who always said they worked at something but never really applied themselves. They played all night and slept it off all day. The first group was by far the largest, but it was the last group that made the most noise and earned for Montparnasse the intriguing but misleading reputation as a place where people dissipated themselves and frittered away their time and talent." —MORRILL CODY

"Such the Montparnasse we knew: a weird little land crowded with artists, alcoholics, prostitutes, pimps, poseurs, college boys, tourists, society slummers, spendthrifts, beggars, homosexuals, drug addicts, nymphomaniacs, sadists, masochists, thieves, gamblers, confidence men, mystics, fakers, paranoiacs, political refugees, anarchists, 'Dukes' and 'Countesses,' men and women without a country; a land filled with a gaiety sometimes real and often feigned, filled with sorrow, suffering, poverty, frustration, bitterness, tragedy, suicide. Not only was there never any place like it; Montparnasse itself had never been before and never will be again what it was in the 1920s.

For it was essentially a part of the first aprés-guerre, and from 1929 on it began dying."

—Samuel Putnam

"And as for the 'Lost Generation' tag, we were no more lost than those who remained at home. We were simply better off in mind and spirit."

—Morrill Cody

"To know Paris is to know a great deal."

—Henry Miller

"The chief danger about Paris is that it is such a strong stimulus, and like most stimulants incites to rushing about and produces a pleasant illusion of great mental activity rather than the solid results of hard work."

—T. S. Eliot

"It was a place where the very air was impregnated with the energies of art."

—Thomas Wolfe

"When spring comes to Paris the humblest mortal alive must feel that he dwells in paradise."

—Henry Miller

"To have come on all this new world of writing, with time to read in a city like Paris where there was a way of living well and working, no matter how poor you were, was like having a great treasure given to you."

—Ernest Hemingway

ACKNOWLEDGMENTS

AS ALWAYS, I BEGIN WITH MY LITERARY AGENT, ADAM CHROMY of Movable Type Management. Adam's encouragement, guidance, expertise, and friendship are absolutely indispensable. Next, of course, is my editor, Lauren Appleton of TarcherPerigee. We worked together on the revised edition of *To Have and Have Another: A Hemingway Cocktail Companion*, and it was a pleasure to be reunited to work with her again. Lauren's patience, talent, and instincts made it very easy for me to place my trust (and manuscript) in her capable hands. Thanks to Meg Leder and Stephanie Bowen at Perigee for their vision and role in the early stages of the book.

A huge *merci beaucoup!* goes to my good friend Alexandre Gabriel, president of Maison Ferrand, makers of Pierre Ferrand Cognac, Plantation Rum, Citadelle Gin, Pierre Ferrand Dry Curaçao, and other superb products. Alexandre's hospitality during my research visit to Paris was extraordinary. Further, I cannot overestimate the time, resources, and expertise offered to me by Fernando Castellon and Mathieu Sabbagh. This book would be a great deal diminished without their assistance, and the time we spent in Paris was not only of great utility, it was damned fun.

Thank you also to fellow cocktail historians, writers and enthusiasts, and, of course, bartenders, notably François Monti, David Wondrich, Ted "Dr. Cocktail" Haigh, Chall Gray, Noah Rothbaum of *The Daily Beast*, Chris McMillian, Francine Cohen, Cori Paige, Anistatia Miller, Jared Brown, Laura Donnelly, Greg Boehm (CocktailKingdom.com, Mud Puddle Inc.), Alan Moss, Dale DeGroff, Arturo Vera-Felicie, Chuck Taggart, Vincenzo Errico, Eric Witz, Fulvio Piccinino, Matteo Mosetti, Kurt Neumann, Brewster Chamberlin, Gina Haase, and Dean Bartholomew. Special thanks go to Elise Greene, Dan Curtin, and Carlson Klapthor for helping me fine-tune the drink recipes and to Ed Greene and Don Rebsch for their proofreading acumen. And a huge debt of thanks is owed to my dear friend, and tremendous artist, Jill DeGroff, for designing the book's beautiful web page, and to my friend Kevin Sauvage for allowing the use of his lovely Scrilly Cottage, a better writing retreat there never was.

Among the brands and publicists who have been so supportive, thanks go to César Giron and Stéphane Kraxner of the Martell Mumm

Perrier-Jouët division of Pernod-Ricard, Guillaume Lamy of Maison Ferrand, Eric Seed, and Jake Parrott of Haus Alpenz, Michael Cherner and Chris Schmid of Prestige Beverage Group, Elizabeth Colton and Dave Karraker of Gruppo Campari, Donatien Ferrari and Brenton Blanchard of Maison Lejay Lagoute, Caitlin Vartain of Anchor Distilling Co., Sean Bucalo of Lucas Bols U.S.A., Inc., Avery Glasser of Bittermens, Anne Trimbach and Susan Anne Cosgrove of Maison F.E. Trimbach, Matthew Green of Esprit Du Vin, Fine Wine Merchants, Mhairi Voelsgen and Connor Frederickson of BroVo Spirits, Sylvain Dadé of Maison Lejay-Lagoute, Adele Robberstad and Michelle Chernoff of Peter F. Heering/Maison Heinrich, John Troia of Tempus Fugit Spirits, Simon Ford, Jason Kosmas and Malte Barnekow of the 86 Co., Lisa Laird Dunn of Laird and Co., Laura Baddish of the Baddish Group, and Shawn Kelley and Lora Piazza of Pernod-Ricard USA.

With respect to libraries, archival resources, and content/rights owners, I wish to thank James Maynard and the Poetry Collection of the University Libraries, University at Buffalo, the State University of New York; Aaron M. Lisec of the Special Collections Research Center, Morris Library, Southern Illinois University; Emily Arseneau and Richard Lambert at Collectif1806.com, the Exposition Universelle des Vins et Spiritueux; Jean-Frédéric Schall, Anya Prosvetova of AKG Images, Ltd.; Laurie Austin and Clara Snyder of the John F. Kennedy Presidential Library and Museum; Diana Reeve of Scala Archives/Art Resource; Kelly Dyson of the U.S. Library of Congress; AnnaLee Pauls of the Firestone Library/Rare Books and Special Collections, Princeton University; Eleanor Lanahan of the F. Scott Fitzgerald Smith Trust, Morgan Stanley.

In Paris, I wish to thank Colin Peter Field, Anita Cotter, and everyone at the Paris Ritz, Harry's New York Bar, Jean-Philippe Levavasseur at the Café la Coupole, Café Sélect, Le Dôme, Yves Esposito at La Closerie des Lilas, the Café de Flore, Serge Girard and the Café de la Rotonde, Brasserie Lipp, Café le Deux Magots, Le Boeuf sur le Toit, Jessica Elineau of Les Grandes Brasseries—Groupe Flo, owners of Le Bouef sur le Toit, Amanda Victoria, Yves Mathieu at Le Lapin Agile, Christophe Davoine at the Hôtel de Crillon, and the research staff at the Bibliothèque Nationale de France. Further, I am greatly indebted to the two amazing online libraries of vintage cocktail books, the Exposition Universelle des Vins et Spiritueux (euvs-vintage-cocktail-books.cld.bz/), as well as Collectif: 1806 (collectif1806.com).

And last, sincere thanks to John Hemingway for interrupting his busy writing schedule to pen my foreword. *Mille grazie, mio fratello! Salute!*

INDEX

Bold indicates names of featured drinks; *i* indicates illustration; *n* indicates
footnote

T

U

V

W

ABOUT THE AUTHOR

Philip Greene is an attorney, writer, and cocktail historian. He is Trademark and Internet Counsel to the U.S. Marine Corps, based at the Pentagon. He is one of the founders of the Museum of the American Cocktail in New Orleans. He has presented at cocktail, wine, and related events around the world.

Philip is the author of two books: *To Have and Have Another: A Hemingway Cocktail Companion* (TarcherPerigee, 2012, 2nd ed. 2015) and *The Manhattan: The Story of the First Modern Cocktail* (Sterling Epicure, 2016) and a contributing columnist for *The Daily Beast*.

He lives in Washington, DC, with his wife, Elise, and (when they visit) three daughters.